3

QUESTIONS

A powerful grid
to help you live
by the grace of God

ROD LOY

InfluenceResources.com

Published by Influence Resources
1445 N. Boonville Ave., Springfield, Missouri 65802

Published in association with The Quadrivium Group—Orlando, FL
info@TheQuadriviumGroup.com

Cover design by interior formatting by Anne McLaughlin
of Blue Lake Design, Dickinson, Texas.
Edited by Jeanne Van Tim.

Note: To protect the anonymity of some of the people in the stories, names and details
have been changed.

ISBN: 978-1-93669-915-5
First printing 2011

Printed in the United States of America

WHAT PEOPLE ARE SAYING ABOUT 3 QUESTIONS . . .

The three questions Rod Loy asks in this book will confront you at the very core of your being and help you discover the person God meant you to be. This is a must-read for those desperate disciples of Christ who are hungry to find the secret to contentment.
—Scott Wilson, Senior Pastor of The Oaks Fellowship, Red Oak, Texas, and author of *Act Normal*

For Christians wanting deeper peace and daily victory in their walk with God, the answer is *3 Questions*. Rod Loy's book uses a trio of soul-searching principles from the Apostle Paul to create a simple, powerful guide that takes believers into profound fellowship with the Lord.
George Wood, General Superintendent Assemblies of God USA, Springfield, Missouri, Author of *Road Trip Leadership*

I've known Rod Loy since his high school days. Reading about his journey in *3 Questions* brought back many memories. I've had a front row seat for the adventure of God's grace in his life. This is a challenging book. If you're tired of business as usual, wondering where to find lasting fulfillment and looking for a way to make your life count, start reading. These three questions will change your life!
—Dr. J. Don George, Founding Pastor Calvary Church, Irving, Texas

In *3 Questions*, Rod Loy breaks through conventional thinking about life and God. He challenges us to genuinely experience grace-not just talk about it. I highly recommend you read his book and let God's Spirit radicalize your life.
—Tommy Barnett, Senior Pastor of Phoenix First Assembly of God, Phoenix, Arizona

Most people think of grace as an abstract idea, but Rod Loy shows us there's nothing more practical! His book offers powerful insights that make God's grace central to our lives rather than just a part of our beliefs. If you want to live the grace of God, get this book.
—Earl Creps, Church Planter and Author of *Reverse Mentoring*, Berkley, California

In *3 Questions*, Rod Loy takes the words of Paul written to the Galatians and redirects them to our hearts today. As a leader, these questions challenge me personally. As a pastor, I want my church to consider the impact their answers to these questions have in their lives. Rod's personal journey in discovering his answers will help you find a path to a more authentic and healthy relationship with Jesus and help you become the person and leader you were meant to be. If you're afraid of what your answers might be, don't pick up this book, but if you're willing to take a risk and evaluate your journey, this is the book for you.
—Tommy Sparger, Lead Pastor of North Point Church, Springfield, Missouri

In *3 Questions*, Rod Loy leads us on a thought-provoking journey. With terrific stories and clear Biblical teaching, he helps us truly appreciate God's grace and discover what it really means to live in His grace. This book provides a great framework to pursue a strong, vibrant walk with Christ.
—Rob Clancy, Senior Vice President and Treasurer, Windstream Corporation

Rod Loy has his finger on the spiritual pulse of our culture. He knows that we want to be able to say that we've done enough to earn points with God. In *3 Questions*, Rod takes us into Paul's letter to the Galatians to show (again) that we begin and end with the grace of God. We can't earn it, and we don't deserve it. But when we experience the unconditional love of Jesus, He transforms our lives from the inside out. If you read Rod's book, it'll change your life.
—John McKinzie, Lead Pastor of Hope Fellowship Church, Frisco, Texas

Missionaries are not exempt from faulty motives, misunderstanding the beautiful terror of grace, the folly of self-reliance, and the inability to speak the truth in love. In *3 Questions*, Rod Loy addresses these essential issues with candor, wisely illustrating how joyful living starts by asking the right questions. I have been both challenged by the self-delusion Rod's thinking exposes and encouraged by the Biblical solutions he articulates. Every missionary ought to read this book.
—Dick Brogden, Missionary in Sudan

Rod Loy's book, *3 Questions,* is a different way to approach life, ministry and leadership. In a culture obsessed with bigger, better, faster and more, Rod offers a different approach—one that will bring freedom, peace and grace to your life. I've known Rod for twenty years and have watched him re-order his life, drop out of the competition and focus on pleasing God first. It's a huge challenge I dare you to take! Instead of seeking simple answers, ask yourself these three questions. Allow God to challenge your motives and priorities. You will be changed.
—Alton Garrison, Assistant Superintendent of the Assemblies of God, Springfield, Missouri

If you're wrestling with the process of redirection in your life or organization—and who isn't?—this is a must-read book. Rod Loy is notorious for making the impossible look easy, which is why it's no surprise that this book is deeply biblical and uniquely balanced. Asking the *3 Questions* is now part of my daily routine. I dare you to give it a try.
—Jason Taylor, Lead Pastor of Faith Assembly Church, Houston, Tex

Wow! I finished the book today. It's amazing, and it truly affected me. I feel like this book was written directly to me to combat my striving for success with the power of God's magnificent grace. Rod's leadership and mentorship have been a game-changer in my life as a husband, as a father, and especially as a church planter in Los Angeles. When I was in the midst of great risk and uncertainty, and the pressure seemed to be too much to handle, these principles helped lead me back to a wonderful joy and trust in Jesus. I wish I could put *3 Questions* in the hands of everyone I know, to read, re-read, and memorize this powerful grid that will empower them to live by God's life-changing grace.

—Nathan Kollar, Lead Pastor of Clarity Church, Los Angeles, California

On January 23, 2011, I launched Resound Church in Portland, Oregon, with over 360 people in attendance. Rod Loy didn't just give me "good advice" about planting a church. His wisdom was instrumental in my personal walk, leadership and in how to reach a lost city. *3 Questions* communicates the heart and perspective God has given Rod. It answers our most fundamental questions pertaining to life and leadership.

—Luke Reid, Church Planter and Pastor of Resound Church, Portland, Oregon

Simple in principle yet profound in practice, *3 Questions* provides the lens we need to correct our myopic view of ourselves and others. Rod has given us the prescription that allows us to share God's 20/20 vision.

—Donna Hill, Vice President of Student Affairs, College of the Ouachitas, Malvern, Arkansas

God has gifted Rod Loy with a remarkable ability to take complex truths from the Word of God and distill them into everyday life. His willingness to reveal his heart and his hurts opens the door for each of us to be honest about our own heart issues. This book is a great tool for small groups or personal study. The best part is that Rod's life is a demonstration of what he writes.

—Darius Johnston, Senior Pastor, Christ Church Assembly of God, Ft. Worth, Texas

I am so pleased Pastor Rod has written *3 Questions*. He has a unique message for the church and for the lost: We must embrace Jesus' grace and share it. Pastor Rod has personally modeled the love and grace of God, both in the good times and difficult ones. When I lost a statewide political race in 2006, he embraced me just as though I had won. He has helped me understand that whether we are receiving the applause of people or their scorn, we must live for the applause of heaven. I believe the readers of this book will sense from Pastor Rod what I have for nearly nineteen years—I can be an instrument of God's grace and help my community move toward the love of God.

—Jay Martin, Attorney at Law, Pastor of Metro Worship Center, Little Rock, Arkansas

3 Questions is a heart-searching book that will help you evaluate your walk with God and His mission for your life. Rod Loy is one of those unique pastors who believes the Gospel is for every Tribe, Tongue and Nation, and has grown a church with a great zeal for the world. I highly recommend his book to you.

—D. Wendel Cover, Pastor of Word of Life International Church, Springfield, Virginia

Pastor Rod Loy has made a very significant investment in my life and has become a valued mentor and friend. He personally challenged me to think about these three questions before it became a book, so I know that they have been stirring in him for a long time. Answering the *3 Questions* changed Rod, and I'm so thankful he challenged me to take the time to answer them, too. It has made me a better follower of Christ, husband, father, friend, and servant leader. I dare you to pick up this book and honestly answer these questions. You'll never be the same, and I guarantee you'll share it with others.

—John Jay Wilson, Leadership Networks, Director of Church Multiplication Network, Springfield, Missouri

Rod Loy's book clearly "schools " us on the importance of following the commandments of God. It's a must read for those who sincerely want to please Him. I believe the Holy Spirit, our teacher, gave him this inspirational book to show us that pleasing God should be our personal goal.

—Rosie Coleman, Administrative Director of Elementary Education, North Little Rock School District

When all is said and done, what really matters is what God thinks of how I have used my life. Rod Loy grapples with three questions that help us develop a life that is pleasing to God. This is a great book, with applicable principles to reorient our lives with a focus on what's important to God.
—Scott Hanson, Missionary, Dar Es Salaam, Tanzania

Rod always challenges me. Whether I see him speaking from the pulpit to thousands, or patiently mentoring one of my young employees at his "real world" job (lifeguarding at our local water park), one thing is always true: He is always asking himself the three questions in this book, and always trying to improve the way he answers them. This book challenges me to do the same.
—Phil Helms, Managing Member, Reve Management, LLC, Little Rock, Arkansas

Many of us are driven to please others in order to be accepted, but in *3 Questions*, Rod Loy shows us clearly that God's acceptance, above all others, is what matters. Pastor Loy's words ring with God's grace and love, and he enriches our lives with the spirit of God's power and presence.
—Mayor Patrick H. Hays, City of North Little Rock, Arkansas

At one time or another, many of us have heard the phrase, "Grace is something we need but don't deserve." In *3 Questions*, Rod Loy provides a refreshing and practical explanation why the grace of God is indispensable in the life of a believer.
—Kermit Bridges, D.Min., President of Southwestern Assemblies of God University, Waxahachie, Texas

Rod Loy is a young leader who has taken a 99 year-old church to new heights. His insights on grace—and a life ordered by grace—will challenge both your priorities and your approach to life. I highly recommend this book to all leaders who are looking for a new "life scoreboard," one filled with meaning and purpose. I'm asking myself the 3 questions every day.

—Larry Moore, Superintendent, Arkansas District of the Assemblies of God, Little Rock, Arkansas

In this book, Rod Loy, a man of transparent sincerity, shows from his experience and wisdom the simple yet often forgotten truths that have the power to change our lives. Three uncomplicated questions, asked and answered honestly, can free us to see our lives, our churches and all of humanity as God intended. The map is printed; it's up to us to live another way, because the greatest men and women of God are simple people who learn how to live the simple truths of Christianity daily!

—Paul Burkhart, Missionary to Laos

This book is dedicated to four mentors who have shaped my life. I'm honored to have served with each of you.

Pastor Darius Johnston.
When I was still a misfit, you saw potential! Thanks for investing your life in a high school student who was ready to learn.

Dr. J. Don George.
You will always be my pastor. Thank you for providing countless meals, opening your home to me, and making me part of your family. You taught me how to serve with excellence.

The late Rev. Dan Rothwell.
Pastor Dan taught me to pray. His prayer life and commitment were an inspiration that challenged me to rely on God.

Dr. Alton Garrison.
Your mentoring continues to shape my life and ministry. Thanks for pouring countless hours of leadership lessons into me.

CONTENTS

ACKNOWLEDGEMENTS

I want to thank my church family at First Assembly. You've been our best friends and biggest supporters for the last nineteen years. Serving with you is a joy and an honor. Thanks for pushing me to write and allowing time for me to do so.

A big thanks to my friend, Pat Springle. You are an incredible resource to the Body of Christ! Thanks for pulling the words out of me and helping me put them on paper.

Thanks to my mom and dad, Dick and Georgia Loy, who continue to wonderfully model God's grace and unconditional love.

Thanks to my boys, Tyler and Parker, for being a constant source of stories and illustrations. I love you and am so proud of you.

Finally, thanks to my wife, Cindy. You are a living example of God's grace. You ordered your life by these questions long before me. Thanks for leading the way and for your exceeding patience with my journey.

1

OUTRAGEOUS GRACE

I am astonished that you are so quickly deserting the one who
called you to live in the grace of Christ and are turning to a
different gospel—which is really no gospel at all. Evidently
some people are throwing you into confusion and are trying to
pervert the gospel of Christ.

was devastated. I put my head down on my desk to hide. I
wanted to cry, but I couldn't let anyone see me doing that. As
I buried my face in my hands, I came to a fierce, determined commitment: I'll never be *that guy* again!

When I was a kid, I was a misfit, a nerd, a geek. No matter what label anyone pinned on me, it amounted to the same
evaluation. I was a loser. By the time I reached junior high school,
my hormones failed to transform me into Brad Pitt. I wore thick
glasses, I had unruly hair, I was skinny, and I read a book a day. I
went to the public library every week and checked out the maxi-
mum books allowed. I always carried a stack of books with me
wherever I went. I read anything that had a cover: novels, history,
and biographies. When I finished a test or assignment, I didn't

talk to other kids. I read the book I'd picked for that day. Books were my security blanket—that's not exactly the prescription for "the most popular kid in class." To no one's surprise, I was painfully shy. I was well aware that I didn't fit in. I was so socially backward that I worried myself sick if a teacher assigned me to read a book report to the class. Quite often, I got sick to my stomach and begged my mom to let me stay home that day.

A kid in our neighborhood picked on me almost every day when we walked home after school. He knocked books out of my hands, laughed as I picked them up, and then knocked them out of my hands again. It was a great sport for him. I didn't want to fight him for several reasons. I was so awkward and thin that I was sure he'd beat me to a pulp, and if my glasses fell off, I'd be almost blind. My eyesight was 20/400 without my Coke-bottle lenses.

One day in gym class, Coach Martin told me to wrestle the biggest, strongest kid on the school football team. I was fairly athletic, but I weighed about as much as a gnat, and I was totally devoid of confidence. As soon as Coach Martin told us to get on the mat, the other boys in the class hooted and hollered because they were sure I was going to get creamed. The big guy didn't pin me, but I was hurt far worse by all the laughs at my expense.

In Mr. Sellent's algebra class, I sat behind the most beautiful girl in junior high, Beth Grayson. She was 5' 4" with short brown hair and a pretty smile. Everybody wanted to be her friend . . . including me. I daydreamed about her—not about having a romantic relationship, but only about being her friend. I knew if I could be *her* friend, everyone else would accept me, too. One day in class, I tapped her on the shoulder and whispered, "Beth, do you have an extra pencil? I forgot mine today."

She turned around and glared at me. Her words dripped with venom: "Don't talk to me. I don't talk to people like you."

That was a defining moment of my life. I knew I wasn't the most popular boy in the school, and I was aware people avoided me, but I had no idea that Beth Grayson found me repulsive. Every fiber of my heart was utterly crushed. I wanted to cry, but I restrained my tears. In that moment of stark, horrible revelation, I made a solemn vow to change my life so I'd never experience this kind of shame again.

> Immediately, I went on a quest to become a different person. I wanted to change to make myself acceptable.

Immediately, I went on a quest to become a different person. I wanted to change to make myself acceptable. The best way to win people over, I quickly concluded, was to make them laugh. I picked three people whose communication skills I wanted to copy. I studied what they said and how they said it. I noticed what they did that got the most laughs, and I observed how they used pauses for dramatic effect. When I got their patterns down, I practiced incessantly. I studied Johnny Carson because he was a master at creating comic tension. Johnny also was the best ever at "saves"— when something that was supposed to be funny didn't work, he made it even more funny. I carefully observed Pee Wee Herman because he can make ordinary things very funny. And I scrutinized David Letterman to see how he creatively talks about a single object for twenty minutes and makes it all hilarious.

Underneath the smiles and jokes was a very hurt, confused, and lonely young man. All the hurt hadn't gone away. It was buried, and it festered into a deep resentment that couldn't be contained. After I acquired my new communication skills, I started hanging out with two friends who thought I'd become pretty cool. We played a game. We stood in the hall, and one of us pointed to an unsuspecting kid. All three of us then engaged the kid in conversation with the expressed purpose of making him cry. In fact, the one who made him cry was the winner. The rules were that we couldn't touch him. We only used words to cut, hack, and bludgeon the victim's soul. And we became quite good at it.

Gradually, I won some respect for being funny. The combination of a fairly quick wit, daily practice, and grim determination gave me the ability to come up with some good laughs. I was sure that if I could make people laugh, they'd accept me. I'd given up on Beth, but there was a whole world of people I could try to impress. I won a lot of them in the next few years, but there was one significant casualty—me. By trying to become someone else, I completely lost my identity. Before I determined to change, I hadn't liked who I was, but now I didn't even know who I was.

MEASURING STICKS

A few years later, my measuring stick changed. I realized making people laugh or cry probably wasn't going to get me very far in life, so I established different standards for success. I studied hard, worked hard, and did everything I could do to prove to others and to myself that I was somebody. When I was eighteen, I made a list of the things I wanted to accomplish by the time I was thirty-five. If I could reach those, I was sure I'd feel great about myself. A few years later, I'd checked off every box on my list, but something very strange happened: I still felt lousy. Each time I reached a goal and realized it didn't give me the thrill I'd expected, I set it higher.

I graduated from college in three years. It was a way to prove I was an achiever. You'd think that I would have learned my lessons by the time I became a pastor, but we have mixed motives just like everyone else. I set a goal for our church to reach two thousand people. When we got there, it wasn't enough, so I targeted twenty-five hundred . . . then three thousand.

Finally, I realized there had to be something more fulfilling. I desperately wanted to find the answer so I could get off the treadmill of setting standards higher and higher but feeling rotten about them even when I achieved them. God led me to Paul's letter to the Galatians, and as I read it, I saw three questions that pierced my heart. These questions formed a new way for me to think about life. They caused me to rethink what's important, examine my motives, and discover what's really important to God and to me. As an outstanding teacher, Paul uses many questions to stimulate his readers to think more deeply, but three stand out:

> These questions formed a new way for me to think about life. They caused me to rethink what's important, examine my motives, and discover what's really important to God and to me.

"Am I now trying to win the approval of human beings, or of God? Or am I trying to please people?" (1:10)

The first question addresses *our motive.* Who are we living for? Who deserves our love and loyalty?

"Are you so foolish? After beginning by means of the Spirit, are you now trying to finish by means of the flesh?" (3:3)

The second question focuses on *our source of power and wisdom*. Do we trust our own abilities, or do we depend on the One who bought us?

"Have I now become your enemy by telling you the truth?" (4:16)

The last question surfaces *our willingness to speak truth* to the people around us. Most people are glad to hear our words of affirmation, but when we find the courage to speak hard words of truth, they may fiercely resist us. Our courage to step up and tell them the truth, though, is an open door for real change in their lives.

In this book, we're going to explore these three questions so they become imbedded in our minds and hearts. When they do, they'll become a valuable template to help us make course corrections each day in order to stay on track with God and His best for our lives. But first, we need to understand why Paul asked these questions. The Galatian believers had a problem . . . a big problem.

NEW RULES

Anyone who reads Paul's letter to the Galatian Christians instantly realizes this letter is very different from his other letters to the believers. Paul is really angry with them. Throughout the letter, his tone is like a loving dad whose teenager has just done something really stupid. He affirms his love at the same time as he gets in their face!

Galatia was a region of modern Turkey, not just a single city. It was about the size of Arkansas. Paul had visited several of the cities there on his first journey to take the gospel to the Roman world. When God used Paul and Barnabas to perform miracles in Lystra, the crowd tried to proclaim them as gods. Paul would have nothing of it and gave glory to God. But in a dramatic switch, people came from Antioch and Iconium and convinced the crowd that Paul and Barnabas were traitors, so the people of Lystra tried to kill them! It shows you how quickly people can switch. In a matter of minutes, they went from hearing "You're a God" to "Kill Him!" They stoned Paul and left him for dead outside the city. When he was revived, he got up and went back to tell more people about Jesus. In every city, Paul faced verbal ridicule and physical attacks. His investment in the people of Galatia was huge. He had spent himself emotionally, physically, and spiritually to help them experience the transforming grace of God. When he got word they'd walked away from Jesus, he was ticked off.

What had happened? After he left their region, a group of people known as Judaizers came to town and convinced the people that all the stuff Paul had said about grace wasn't the real picture. They said, "If you want to really walk with God, you need to follow the commands in the Bible. Follow them, and you're in; don't follow them, and you're out." The commands in the Bible are called "the law of God." God's laws were given to His people for several purposes: to show them His standard of holiness, to point them to grace because they (and we) can't measure up to His standards on our own, and to remind them (and us) how to live as believers. There are over six hundred commands in the Old Testament, covering issues as broad as diet, sacrifice, marriage, worship, and every other aspect of life. In addition, the religious leaders of Jesus' day added thousand more rules for people to follow. Today, when we talk about laws, we usually are referring to traffic regulations, the protection of life and property, or state and federal legislation. Law, standards, or rules—the terms are interchangeable, but if we choose to live by them, we never escape their oppressive power. No matter how many we follow, there are always some we forget each day. They're like the massive notebook that comes with a new software program. Countless glitches can happen because we're unaware of the intricacies of the code. If we live by the laws, we're always looking over our shoulder to see if God or anyone else will catch us failing—and failure is inevitable.

> If we live by the laws, we're always looking over our shoulder to see if God or anyone else will catch us failing—and failure is inevitable.

Some people might say that in our postmodern culture, we're relativists: "You can determine your own rules and reality, but don't tell me what I have to believe or do. I'm creating my own rules." Apart from grace, people gravitate to rules to define themselves. If they don't use the rules of God, their parents, or their club, they create their own. I know a young man who has completely rejected the rules of his parents' home and his church. He insists he's free, but he lives by the unwritten but rigid rules of the drug culture: Get high, defy authority, have as much sex as you can get, and trust no one but each other. Living in the drug culture, this young man has adapted to its standards of clothing, language, finances, relationships, and behavior. This culture has very clear rules, and it uses ridicule and rejection to punish those who don't follow them.

No one lives apart from some concept of right and wrong. These concepts are the rules that determine our values, our relationships, and our choices.

When Paul toured the cities of Galatia, he explained that believing in the gospel of Jesus Christ isn't a commitment to follow all the rules in the Old Testament. Anyone with an ounce of self-awareness will admit he can't measure up to God's standards—but there's One who did. Jesus met the standard of perfection and stood in our place to pay the penalty we rightly deserve. It's called grace.

The concept of grace is one of the most revolutionary ideas in all of history. The ancient Roman world knew nothing of it. People rose if they had power, and they fell without it. People valued military might and financial strength. The idea of loving the unlovely and accepting the unacceptable was unthinkable. But that's what Jesus did.

Today, people have some common misconceptions about grace. We sometimes talk about "saying grace" at meals as if it's a meaningless ritual. Some of us who are a little older remember Grace Kelly, the Princess of Monaco, who was the epitome of elegance, beauty, and grace. But the most common misunderstanding of grace is that it's a warm, sweet, syrupy feeling we get from thinking about God. I'd like to propose a different view, one that Paul communicated everywhere he went: *Grace is a stunning rescue of helpless people.* Who does God rescue? Good people who have earned it? Not at all. Those who have jumped through a church's hoops? No, missed it again. People who have tried really hard to make themselves acceptable to God? No. Trying hard results in prideful self-righteousness if we do pretty well, or it produces shame when we repeatedly fail to live up to the standards.

Who is the person Jesus saves? The one who admits he has fallen, is flawed, and is completely helpless to win God's approval on his own. How big a deal is sin? A really big deal! Paul wrote the to the Romans that "the wages of sin is death" (Romans 6:23). That means what we rightly deserve for our sins is the death of separation from God's love and presence. Today, people wink at selfishness and laugh at sin. We may agree that murder is wrong, but we rationalize almost everything short of that. Most of us instinctively have a list of sins we keep in our minds. And we categorize the sins. There are really bad sins, bad sins, kind of bad sins, and sins we don't really count because we enjoy doing them. As long as we don't do the really bad ones (or don't do them too often), we feel pretty good about ourselves. But moving the benchmark of acceptable behavior doesn't deal with the fundamental problem of human depravity. We can't save ourselves no matter how hard we try. And sin isn't just breaking some set of arbitrary rules—it's breaking the heart of God.

Too often, people try to view the Christian faith through one of two lenses: being moral enough to earn God's approval or giving up and finding freedom by throwing off all the rules. The gospel isn't a blend or balance of these two; it's a third way. We acknowledge that God's standards are good and right, but we're well aware that we can never measure up. Our sense of failure doesn't drive us to despair—it leads us to the cross where we realize Jesus suffered the death we deserve to die and paid the price we could never pay. Then, out of sheer gratitude for His love and acceptance, we want to please Him in every way we can. Then, God's standards take on a far different meaning. Instead of being steps to try to earn God's acceptance, they become ways we gladly choose to honor the One who rescued us. We don't obey to earn God's love; we obey because we're so thankful for His grace. There's a world of difference. The gospel doesn't do away with God's law, but it infuses the law with a very different purpose. Instead of it creating shame or pride in us, it becomes a directive to help us please our Father.

When we come to God, we come with empty hands and open hearts. If we come with a laundry list of our accomplishments, He's not impressed. But if we come with a broken heart, He warmly welcomes us. Jesus told a story about a tax collector and a Pharisee who went to the temple to pray. Pharisees were the ultimate

> Too often, people try to view the Christian faith through one of two lenses: being moral enough to earn God's approval or giving up and finding freedom by throwing off all the rules. The gospel isn't a blend or balance of these two; it's a third way.

rule-keepers. They felt smug because they followed so many rules so religiously. But tax collectors were at the other end of society's spectrum. They were Jews who collected taxes from their countrymen for the Roman occupiers. People considered them to be traitors, and they hated them. Jesus said these two men went into the temple. The Pharisee prayed, "God, I thank you that I am not like other people—robbers, evildoers, adulterers—or even like this tax collector. I fast twice a week and give a tenth of all I get" (Luke 18:11-12). But the tax collector's heart had been melted by God's grace. He wouldn't even look up. He beat his breast as he prayed, "God, have mercy on me, a sinner" (verse 13).

Jesus explained, "I tell you that this man, rather than the other, went home justified before God. For all those who exalt themselves will be humbled, and those who humble themselves will be exalted" (verse 14).

When Paul was in Galatia, the people had responded to him and his message as the tax gatherer had, with a broken and open heart, but after he left, they had become Pharisees. Paul didn't mince words at the beginning of his letter. The Judaizers had hijacked Paul's message of grace, and to add insult to injury, they had attacked him personally. Paul didn't back down one inch. He fussed at the people, and he warned them to steer clear of the people who had ruined their concept of grace. He wrote:

I am astonished that you are so quickly deserting the one who called you to live in the grace of Christ and are turning to a different gospel—which is really no gospel at all. Evidently some people are throwing you into confusion and are trying to pervert the gospel of Christ. But even if we or an angel from heaven should preach a gospel other than the one we preached to you, let them be under God's curse! As we have already said, so now I say again: If anybody is preaching to you a gospel other than what you accepted, let them be under God's curse! (Galatians 1:6-9)

Can't you picture Paul's face as he wrote these words? He was angry, but it wasn't flippant annoyance. His anger rose out of his deep love for the people who had not only forsaken the freedom and hope of salvation, but had also gone back into the slavery of rules.

Here's my paraphrase of these verses. I think Paul was saying, "You idiots! After I taught you about the love and forgiveness found only in Jesus and you experienced the freedom and joy of His grace, you've turned your back on Him and me. Before I came, you tried to live by a set of rules, but you failed, and you were miserable. Why in the world have you gone back to those rules? There's no joy, no satisfaction, and no fulfillment in trying to keep them—only failure, shame, and bondage. You've gone back to the things Jesus saved you from. Come on! Wake up! You've got a choice to make: It's either grace, Jesus, and me . . . or it's the Judaizers, a long set of rules to follow, and constant guilt because you don't measure up. There's no in between. Pick one or the other, but you'd better pick wisely. Everything depends on your response."

The Pharisees of Jesus' day, the Judaizers in Galatia, and some people around today mistakenly think that they can earn God's acceptance by following enough rules. Of course, the rules they promote are the ones they do pretty well. Here are some conversations we might overhear:

"Do not murder." Check. I haven't killed anybody in weeks.

"Don't commit adultery." Got it. I'm not like *those* people. (But there is that uncomfortable passage in the gospels about lust being comparable to adultery [Matthew 5:27-30]. I'd rather not think about that.)

"Go to church." Well, how often? Every week? A couple of times a month? Yeah, that's good enough.

"Have no other gods." Well, sure. I don't have any statues around my house. Oh, so you're saying that "gods" aren't always statues? If they include success, pleasure, and approval, I've got a problem because I spend far more time pursuing those things than God.

"Don't covet." Oh, come on. Nobody can follow that one. I wish I had a nicer car, a bigger house, a better vacation, a more pleasant spouse, a better body, a higher title, and on and on. Let's move on.

And here's the last one, the Golden Rule: "Do unto others as you would have them do to you." So you're asking me to spend a day, maybe six hours, or even just one hour selflessly, passionately, creatively, and tirelessly meeting the needs of others. Oh, man, I'm not sure I can make it five minutes!

People who try to win acceptance with God and others by following rules have to define which rules and determine how much is good enough. If they even take a glance at their hearts, they quickly see that their motives and secret desires are, at best, mixed. The gospel of Christ never gives us rules as a way to earn God's love, but only as a tool to show us how much we desperately need God's outrageous grace. If we try to follow the rules without grace, we become arrogant and resentful or oppressed by guilt, but if we let the unconditional love and forgiveness of God flood our hearts, we realize we are worth more to God than the stars in the sky, the oil in the ground, and all the diamonds the world has ever produced—not because we've earned this status, but only because it's a free gift from the hand of God.

If Paul were writing you and me today, what would he say? I have a hunch that he might say a lot of the same things to us he said to the Galatians. Why? Because it's so easy for us to begin strong in God's magnificent grace and then drift back to rules to define our spiritual lives. Living by a set of rules (whoever makes the list) can seem more attractive than God's grace for two reasons: They're visible and measurable, and they make us feel good when we meet them. But they always result in spiritual, emotional, and relational poverty—arrogance or shame—instead of gratitude, joy, and affection for God.

> The gospel of Christ never gives us rules as a way to earn God's love, but only as a tool to show us how much we desperately need God's outrageous grace.

"LESS THAN"

In some way and to some degree, all of us feel like misfits. Personal sin and radical insecurity are parts of the human condition. The only people who don't have occasional pangs of conviction and self-doubt are sociopaths—who are the ultimate misfits. We may be skilled academically, athletically, physically, verbally, or professionally, but no amount of success can keep the demons of doubt at bay. We secretly wonder what it'll take next time to win applause, laughs, or hugs. We hope we can do enough to be acceptable to God and to those around us, but we secretly fear that our character flaws and failures will leave us out in the cold.

Every aspect of public life works by creating insecurity. Educators give grades and threaten failure or loss of a scholarship. Politicians try to convince us that "the other guy" is a bum and should be thrown out. Many families run on manipulation, rationalization, and denial instead of honesty and love. They seldom admit it, but they're trying to keep people off balance so they can control them. I actually know a pastor whose stated leadership philosophy is "keep them off balance." If anyone feels too comfortable, he shakes him up because his goal is to create insecure followers. Why? So they'll need him. The most pervasive and powerful force that fosters insecurity in our culture is advertising. It's so common that we don't even notice its effect. How does a company sell toothpaste? By convincing us that its product will not only clean our teeth, but also that whiter teeth and fresh breath will enable us to win friends. Virtually every ad has a surface promise and a subtle, yet powerful hidden promise. The surface promise is that toothpaste will clean your teeth, but the hidden, seductive promise is that this tube of goo will provide the relationships you've longed to enjoy. Without this brand of toothpaste, you run the risk of a meaningless, lonely existence!

Apple is the king of upgrades. I'm amazed at the skill of its advertising strategy. No matter how happy I am with my current Apple computer, I can't wait until the next model comes out. This isn't just an imaginary thirst for more and better computing power. When I go through the scanner at the airport, common, everyday laptops get no attention at all, but if someone sees my Mac laptop, he often says, "Is that the new one? Man, I love those Macs." I always want to be able to say, "Yep, it's the latest model." I don't want to be mortified by having to say, "Uh, no. It's the older version, but I hope to get the new one soon." I'm a willing victim of Apple's intentional upgrade approach. I know it's a strategy, but I still give in to the pressure.

Modern advertising is purposely designed to create discontent so we'll buy a product or use a service to meet our now obvious need. An ad is successful if it makes us feel insecure. It promises us an ideal life of beauty, popularity, riches, power, and comfort, but its idealism is hollow. It drives us to spend money on things—often things we don't even need. It creates insecurity and then promotes products and services to resolve that gnawing feeling of being "less than." Ads in printed media and on billboards, television, and radio want to convince us that we simply have to have a better car, a bigger boat, nicer clothes, a faster computer, better seats at the ball game, a tastier hamburger, a more luxurious vacation, a cooler tattoo, and virtually everything else under the sun that companies want to market and sell. Companies that promise security, like financial services companies, include the implicit threat of ruin or shame if we don't use their services. In some cases, the money pumped into marketing a product is far more than the production cost of the item being sold, so the cost doubles because of the massive ad budget. That's how important and powerful advertising is in our culture.

We have an innate quest for meaning and security. When we feel insecure, however, we often go in the wrong direction in a vain pursuit. We try to fill our lives with things, pleasure, sex, drugs, success at work, sports, beauty, or anything else that promises to fill the hole in our hearts. When I was a kid, my deep, gnawing insecurity didn't push me into drugs, alcohol, or premarital sex. Instead, I tried to win approval through the power of humor. To some degree, my efforts were successful—I became more popular—but at a staggering cost of even greater insecurity because I never really knew if the people who laughed loved my great lines or me. (Actually, I knew they'd drop me like a hot rock if I wasn't funny—a realization that kept driving me to be as funny as I could possibly be, no matter who was the brunt of my jokes.)

> When we feel insecure, however, we often go in the wrong direction in a vain pursuit. We try to fill our lives with things, pleasure, sex, drugs, success at work, sports, beauty, or anything else that promises to fill the hole in our hearts.

Insecurity isn't the real culprit; our wrong solutions to our feelings of self-doubt cause the problems. If our insecurity has driven us to the love, forgiveness, and acceptance of God, it has been a wonderful and constructive path in our lives. But far too often, we take the wrong fork in the road. We try to fill our lives with anything but God and experience devastating effects. Let me describe a few wrong paths:

We try to escape the painful feelings.

We use television, drugs, alcohol, sex, work, pornography, food, gambling, and other substances and behaviors to numb the pain and provide some stimulation to an empty life. We do whatever it takes to escape the hurt. Strangely, some people cut themselves to relieve pain. Their explanation is that the pain they feel from the knife or razor takes their minds off the more searing pain of abuse or abandonment. Some kids and adults play video games for endless hours each day to fill the inner void. If they can keep their minds busy, they don't have to think about the emptiness gnawing at them. Through pornography (now, increasingly for women as well as for men), people want to feel some sense of connection with people they don't know and can't touch because they feel disconnected from the people they are around every day. In countless ways, people try to escape their painful emotions.

We please people so they'll accept us.

We look in the faces of people each day, and we long to see them smile at us. To win their approval at home, at work, and in our friendships, we carefully craft our words and actions to suit them. These people become our mirrors. The look on their faces tells us that we're either safe and secure, detestable, or even worse, not worth their time to even notice us. Our identity is wrapped around their smiles or frowns. Some of us have become "hyper-vigilant," carefully listening to others' voice inflections and watching for the slightest change in facial expressions so we can alter our behavior to please them. Only if they smile, do we feel secure, but even then, we wonder, *What about next time?*

We're driven to achieve.

Some of us are driven to succeed at all cost. In business, academics, sports, cooking, and anything else we attempt, we have to be on top. We may want to prove to others that we belong in an organization, or we may be proving to ourselves that we can make it. Some of us are determined to convince others they're wrong about us. They predicted we'd fail, and our attitude is, "I'll show them!" When winning is in the center of our identity, we end up using people as the next steppingstone instead of loving them for who they are and helping them succeed.

We hide and wear disguises.

When I felt so lonely in junior high, I retreated to the safety of books. I knew they couldn't hurt me, and they gave me momentary pleasure. Later, I tried a very different tactic. I transformed myself into a comedian and wore a mask to cover my true identity, all day, every day. People hide by withdrawing to their bedroom, or they hide in plain sight behind a phony identity. They try to project a confident, secure, untouchable façade, but that's all it is: a shell of a person. We want to convince people we're capable and happy, but we're dying inside. Sadly, some people go into marriage wearing a mask instead of being authentic. When the real person surfaces sooner or later, it's a shock to the spouse and sometimes destroys the marriage. The loneliest people are those who hide behind masks. They long for people to love them for who they are, but they're too afraid to let anyone know them. Somewhere in the past, they concluded, *If people really knew me, they wouldn't like me.* If we wear a mask long enough, we may get to a point when it becomes fused to our faces and we don't know who we are anymore. At that moment, we feel completely lost, but our loneliness is coupled with confusion and hopelessness.

We change the standards so we can meet them.

Some people try to meet a set of expectations—their own or someone else's—but when they fail, they simply change the rules so they can meet them. This is done in our schools, elevating grades so that almost everyone makes an A. This is also done in parenting. I've talked to parents who have given up on training their teenagers to be responsible young adults. Instead of being diligent to impart values and holding their kids to honorable behavior, these parents offer plenty of excuses for their children's misbehavior: "Everybody's doing it." "It doesn't hurt anybody." "I don't want to be judgmental." "He'll grow out of it." For most of us, the standards we set for ourselves and our families have been crafted by watching someone we respect. However, when these standards prove hard to reach, we find someone else to copy, someone with lower expectations and looser standards. There's nothing wrong with finding someone to emulate. Paul told the church in Corinth, "Follow my example as I follow the example of Christ" (1 Corinthians 11:1). The essence of the Christian faith is "keeping our eyes on Jesus." The problem is that most of us keep our eyes on someone else.

We simply give up.

Some people have tried so long, failed so often, and felt so helpless that they've simply throw in the towel and given up on life. They've concluded, *I am what I am, and I'll never be able to measure up.* A deep, poisonous sense of shame whispers to them

a thousand times a day, *You're nothing, and nobody cares about you.*
They try to fill their day with entertainment or mindless activities
so they don't have to think and feel—because thinking reminds
them of their failures and their emotions are so pervasively painful. People simply can't live without at least a kernel of hope. Hope
is "a happy anticipation of a desired future." It only takes a little
to give us the energy and direction we need to take steps forward
each day. We aren't selectively depressed. When we give up in one
area of our lives, it affects every other part.

THE PARADOX OF GRACE

The gospel of Christ is inside out and upside down. Jesus
welcomed the ones who were outside—misfits, tax collectors,
prostitutes, children, the lame, and the blind. But the religious
insiders—the Pharisees, the Sadducees, and the religious elite—
were left out because they were too arrogant to admit their need
for a Savior. God's grace is the most magnificent gift the world
has ever known, but we have to admit our emptiness in order
to be filled with it. Through the prophet Jeremiah, God put the
condition of the human heart this way:

> *"My people have committed two sins:*
> *They have forsaken me,*
> *the spring of living water,*
> *and have dug their own cisterns,*
> *broken cisterns that cannot hold water" (Jeremiah 2:13).*

We're all thirsty for love and purpose, but too often, we drink
from "broken cisterns" of applause, prestige, comfort, and clout

instead of the only drink that really satisfies. Jesus has an answer to our dilemma. John paints the picture for us at a great festival in Jerusalem where each day's events built to a crescendo:

God's grace is the most magnificent gift the world has ever known, but we have to admit our emptiness in order to be filled with it.

On the last and greatest day of the festival, Jesus stood and said in a loud voice, "Let anyone who is thirsty come to me and drink. Whoever believes in me, as Scripture has said, rivers of living water will flow from within them" (John 7:37-38)

When we admit our lives are barren and all our efforts to twist God's arm have failed, we're ready to drink deeply of Jesus and be filled with the refreshing grace of God. We want it to pour over us, and we're thrilled that Jesus loves us so much. Then, we can't contain ourselves. We look around for someone to thank, and we find Christ. We look around for someone to serve, and we see our family, friends, and neighbors. When the outrageous grace of God fills our hearts, we want to honor Him in every way we can imagine. That's the role of the law for believers—not to earn God's love, but to be so filled with His love that it overflows from us to others.

People instinctively have two powerful goals: to find meaning in life and avoid pain as much as possible. All of our behaviors are designed to accomplish these objectives. Most people have only a glimmer of insight (if any at all) about the methods they use to try to cope with their insecurities. The job of pastors, counselors, parents, and friends is to help people become self-aware so they can make better choices. But the hill is pretty high. People cling to their defenses for several reasons: It's all they've ever known, it has worked to some degree, and it always holds the promise of working next time. Change often comes only when they've tried everything to escape, please, achieve, or hide, but none of it is working any more. Now, they have to face the hard truth . . . which can be the best moment of their lives if they make the right choices. When I tried to wear a mask of being a comedian to impress people and win their approval, I created even more heartache within myself and more distance in my relationships. But when I found the courage to admit I was a misfit, I opened a door to God's grace, and honesty paved the way to far more meaningful relationships.

My junior high experience was very painful, but something lured me back to the school fifteen years later when I was a young adult. On a quiet summer afternoon, I drove up to the school, got out, and asked a janitor to let me go in and walk the halls. I went into the gym and looked at the place where I'd wrestled the big football player. I walked into Mr. Sellent's algebra class and stood next to my desk on the third row. The one in front of it was where Beth Grayson sat. In every room and down every hall, the memories and the emotions came flooding back. Suddenly, I felt like I was thirteen years old again. I collected myself and went back to my car. I got in and put my head on the steering wheel. I'd gained a lot of insight about myself during a decade and a half, but the pain was as fresh and raw as it had been years before. I poured out my heart to the Lord, but I didn't pray, "God, heal this hurt in my heart." Yes, I know that's what most people pray, but instead,

I prayed, "Lord, never let me forget how this feels. I want to re-member this pain for the rest of my life so that I have compassion for other people like me—those who are misfits, unwanted, fail-ures, rejected, and forgotten. Help me remember so I'll care for the people who matter to You and love them the way You love them. God, help me remember."

This was another pivotal point in my life. Sometimes, when I tell my story, a well-meaning person will come up to me and sug-gest, "Rod, you need to ask God to release you from your past." But I don't want God to release me from it. He has done incred-ible work to heal the hurts and use the pain to teach me lessons, but I never want to forget the pain. It's the fuel to enable me to care for people who believe no one will ever love them. Not long ago, a young girl asked to speak to me after I taught at a retreat. She poured out her heart and told me about her loneliness and confusion. I gave her a big hug and both of us cried. I knew how she felt, and even more important, she knew I knew how she felt. I didn't have to give her "ten principles to heal life's hurts." I only needed to be there and care.

MY HOPE FOR YOU

God has used Paul's letter to the Galatians in a powerful way in my life, and I hope He does the same for you. Before we dive into the three questions, we needed to first get a good grasp of God's grace. Only then can we answer these questions appro-priately. These three questions have become a grid for me. I ask them every day to remind me of what's most important, where my security is found, the source of my strength, and the way to relate to the people I love. I hope you'll use them this way, too.

As I grow stronger and deeper in God's grace, I see every day as a gift from Him. Instead of wading through an oppressive list of demands and expectations each day and striving—and failing—to meet them, I have a new motivation. Earlier in my Christian life, I didn't get it. I still thought I had to jump through enough hoops to win God's approval. It was oppressive. Now, as I let the grace of God fill my heart, I feel that wonderful blend of contentment and passion. I know God loves me and accepts me unconditionally, and this realization spurs me to please Him all day, every day.

At the end of each chapter you'll find some questions to help you think and pray about what you've read. I encourage you to take plenty of time with these. It's not a speed drill, so if you want to think long and hard about a particular issue, stay there as long as you want. It'll be worth the effort. These questions are also designed to be used in classes and groups to stimulate discussion. I trust God will use this book to melt you with His love and mold you to become the person He wants you to be.

CONSIDER THIS . . .

1. Do you think everybody (perhaps secretly) feels like a misfit? Why or why not?

2. What are some of the measuring sticks people use to help them figure out if they're acceptable? What are some of the measuring sticks you use? Which of these seem to offer the most promise?

3. What are some ways people use the word "grace"? Which of these are on track with the gospel's definition? Which ones fall short?

4. Read Galatians 1:6-9. Do you think Paul is too harsh in his words and tone? Explain your answer.

5. Of the ways people try to cope with life when they feel "less than," which ones are most common among people you know? Which ones have you used? What were the results?

6. How would you explain "the paradox of grace"?

7. At this point in your life, are you thrilled with the grace of God, or do you secretly (or not so secretly) still hope you can do enough to measure up and earn God's approval? What are some ways people can measure what they really believe about grace?

8. What do you hope to get out of this book?

2

DANCING ON A STRING

Question #1:

Am I now trying to win the approval of human beings, or of God? Or am I trying to please people?

Rob always had his eye on the next rung up the corporate ladder. Only six years after he graduated from college and was hired by a national mortgage company, he was already a division manager. Others whispered he was "the golden boy" on his way up, and he loved to hear those whispers. He had married Kimberly, a very pretty girl he had met at the university. She fit into his plans very well. She was socially adept, and he made sure she wore the latest fashions at every company event. When he had her on his arm, everyone turned to look.

In every presentation to the CEO and other corporate brass, Rob rehearsed what he'd say and how he'd say it. He wanted to appear spontaneous and make offhand quips, but it was all carefully orchestrated, even down to faked fumbling for some notes.

He didn't want to appear too polished. He became a master at appearing totally relaxed and completely in control. His bosses were always very impressed. At work, he was always the first one to arrive each morning and among the last to leave the parking lot every evening. When his boss asked for a volunteer for a difficult assignment, Rob's hand always went up.

Two years after they married, Rob and Kimberly had a baby. As the little girl grew, she sometimes threw tantrums or pouted. These behaviors didn't fit into Rob's plans for advancement, so he privately barked at Kimberly to make their little girl shape up—especially when company employees and managers were around! Kimberly bought into Rob's corporate climb because she enjoyed the additional income with each promotion and the prestige of being the golden boy's wife. She played the game exceptionally well, crafting her persona as the wife and mother who had it all together. They attended church and made sure they said just the right things to the pastor, and they appeared at every social event in town, looking like the picture of success.

Both Rob and Kimberly had a fantasy future in their minds. They knew how many perfect kids they'd have, the part of town where they'd live when he'd be a vice president, the clubs they'd join, and the full array of perks they'd enjoy. Any setback to their plans upset them. When their daughter was a little slow to walk, Rob complained, and Kimberly tried to prop up the little girl for hours each day. When another young woman had a prettier dress, Kimberly felt personally violated. When another rising star in the company got a big account and plenty of praise from the CEO, Rob unleashed a whisper campaign to discredit him. To them, gaining approval and prestige was a game, but it was one they had to win at all costs. They couldn't see it, but playing this game was ruining their lives.

OUT OF THE WOMB

People who live for approval are like marionettes dancing on a string. In conversations, they "read" every facial expression and every change in voice intonation, and they analyze every interaction to see if the person they desperately want to please is impressed with them. If they are, they feel relieved and energized: It has worked! But if not, they change their words and behavior to win a smile.

> In conversations, they "read" every facial expression and every change in voice intonation, and they analyze every interaction to see if the person they desperately want to please is impressed with them.

From the time we're born, we're grilled with the idea that to make it in life, we have to please people. When parents take their kids to a restaurant, school, or church, or they have friends come over to cook burgers, a kid who doesn't instantly comply with the parents' orders gets the message, "You'd better shape up! What are other people going to think?" Parents compare everything about their kids with their friends' children: what they wear, the grades they make, their athletic accomplishments, their skills in music, their social prowess, their choice of friends, who they date, and on and on and on. Then, when these kids get to high school and they're living for the approval of their peers, their parents are shocked and ask, "If your friends jump off a cliff, would you jump off, too?"

These parents are using their kids' intelligence and skills as a barometer, not of the kids' success, but of the parents' skill to raise "successful children." In this environment, kids are like sponges. They soak up the culture of the family and learn that pleasing people is the highest and most valuable goal in life. What does this look like? The examples are almost endless:

It's the student who goes to a party he knows he shouldn't attend and does things he knows he shouldn't do. He never plans to make a drunken fool out of himself, but everyone is encouraging him to have one more. He makes the decision to please people at the party instead of pleasing God.

It's the young adult who sleeps with her boyfriend because he says he loves her, wants her, and needs her. She knows it's wrong, but she doesn't want him to ditch her and find another girl. She makes the decision to please him instead of pleasing God.

It's the person in business who compromises his standards by going to a strip club after work. On the way over, he rationalizes, How will I ever network and move up if I don't join them? He's more concerned about fitting in than pleasing God.

It's the people who spend money they don't have to impress people they don't even like. But they've convinced themselves they simply must have impressive new stuff or their friends will reject them. Pleasing people can lead to staggering debt.

Quite often, our choices appear innocent, but they have dev-
astating consequences. In a casual conversation that turns to
vicious gossip, we might wonder, didn't mean to be a part of
that kind of talk. I didn't want to gossip. I hated that they were
saying those things, but I joined in, too. Why couldn't I stop?
Our primary goal isn't our integrity or the honor of the person
who is the target of gossip. Our primary purpose is to avoid
looking like a narrow, religious nut to our friends. We choose to
please people instead of pleasing God.

It's why some parents worry so much when their kids go off to
college. They're afraid their son or daughter will make a wrong
decision and make them look bad. These parents are more con-
cerned with their reputation than their child displeasing God.

PULLED

We are thoroughly relational people, and we thrive only in the context of human connections. God has made us that way, and it's not going to change. Of course, personality and temperament profiles show that some of us are more task-oriented than others, but all of us have a built-in need to relate to others. We long for approval, but too often, we pursue the approval of fickle human beings instead of the applause of Almighty God. To some degree, it's understandable: We can see the smile of a family member, friend, or employer—and we're painfully aware of their frowns of disapproval—but we don't see the face of God. Still, the gospel accounts clearly depict the heart of Jesus Christ. As we read these biographies, we understand what makes Him smile.

As Christians, many of us want it both ways. We want to

please God, but just as much or more, we want the affirmation of the people around us. In his letter to the Galatians, Paul said we have to decide which one is more important. After he chastened them for abandoning grace and returning to rules, he defended his authority as their spiritual father and shepherd. He was telling them some hard but necessary facts—truths they didn't want to hear. He was well aware his correction wouldn't make them happy, so he asked, "Am I now trying to win the approval of human beings, or of God? Or am I trying to please people?" And he concluded, "If I were still trying to please people, I would not be a servant of Christ" (Galatians 1:10). There's no middle ground, no ying and yang, no blend and balance. Paul is saying, "You have to choose which is more important to you. If you choose to please people as your Number 1 priority, you're destined to run on a never-ending treadmill of reading people and doing whatever it takes to make them happy with you. You'll win sometimes, but you'll sacrifice the most important relationship of your life, the one that promises the height of meaning and the depth of love. Don't mess this up! Make the right choice."

If our hearts are full of the grace of God, we want to honor and please the One who bought us and freed us from the prison of sin and death. He comes first, and second place is pretty distant. As we please Jesus, we learn to love the way He loved, speak the way He spoke, and serve the way He served. When we treat people with that much respect, we have honest, authentic, real relationships with them. If we put Christ first, we get great relationships with people, too. But if we put people first, we live in fear, we're easily manipulated, and our relationship with God becomes anemic and distorted.

In Jesus' life, some people were thrilled to experience His love, but others despised Him. That's what will happen with us, too. There can only be a single highest priority in our lives—we can either please God with all our hearts or please people with all our hearts. We "can't serve God and mammon," and we can't have two firsts competing for top billing in the center of our souls. It all starts with being so overwhelmed by the grace of God that our desires are transformed.

> If our hearts are full of the grace of God, we want to honor and please the One who bought us and freed us from the prison of sin and death. He comes first, and second place is pretty distant.

Paul's first question focuses on our motives, and we should only ask it of ourselves. We shouldn't go to other people and ask them, "Are you trying to please God or please people?" No, we should take time to search our own hearts and ask if the wonder of God's grace has truly captured us—or not. This is the first and fundamental question that shapes our motivations and the direction of our lives, but it can be phrased in many different ways:

- To whom do I belong?
- Who is worthy of my affections and loyalty?
- Who has a claim on my life?
- Whose cause is worth the investment of all my resources and energies?

Every game has a scoreboard, and this question is the ultimate scoreboard of life: What matters more than anything else? What's the biggest win of life? In the opening paragraphs of his letter to the people in the region of Galatia, Paul says the scoreboard is our desire to put a smile on Jesus' face above all else. All day, every day, we make choices to live for the approval of God or the approval of the people around us. Those choices are the scores we post every single day.

The evaluation of our motives goes far beyond our outward behavior. The Pharisees and Judaizers did a lot of right things, but they did them for wrong reasons—to gain leverage with God and twist people's arms instead of loving God and serving people. The two motives are worlds apart. Wrong motives drive us to manipulate people instead of caring for them. We do a lot of things God wants us to do, but with an ulterior and selfish purpose. How would our lives change if we lived each day for God's approval? How would it change our drives, our relationships, how we spend our time and money, and our responses to the things that bother us? We won't have completely pure motives until we see Jesus face to face, but in the meantime, our goal as believers is to pursue God with every fiber in us and long to please Him above every other pursuit.

We can't blame other people for demanding that we please

How would our lives change if we lived each day for God's approval? How would it change our drives, our relationships, how we spend our time and money, and our responses to the things that bother us?

them. A flawed motive is our problem to solve. A boss or spouse or parent may use our misplaced goal of being a pleaser, but the fact that we dance on the string of approval and disapproval is our fault, and it's our choice to change.

WRONG ANSWERS

We often analyze our lives and conclude that we simply have to work harder and smarter to win the approval of people. Our wrong conclusion leads us to three strategies that promise love and joy but are counterproductive. These include:

Self-promotion

Some people incessantly talk about themselves. In every conversation, they tell others about their latest deal, acquisition, or victory. They live by the dictum: If you don't toot your own horn, no one will toot it for you. They're committed to extending their own brand by marketing their abilities and wit to anyone who'll listen—and to quite a few who don't want to hear it! The classic self-promoter is Donald Trump. He doesn't care what people say about him as long as they're saying his name. He says outrageous things to get the attention of the media. Even if he's a laughingstock, he's happy to be the center of attention. Most of us don't go to this extreme, but we can't stand it when others get applause. We may smile, but secretly, we envy the attention the person has received. We feel violated, and we double our efforts to win approval the next time. Junior high students haven't learned the relational savvy to be discreet, so they talk non-stop about themselves. They run up and announce, "Hey, did you see what I did? I can't wait to show you!" Athletes call press conferences to highlight their accomplishments and explain how they're indispensable to their team. In college, graduate school, business, and clubs, we call it marketing. Self-promotion is a vital tool for those who insist on pleasing people to fill the hole in their hearts.

Self-promoters are always thinking about how they can angle for more attention. They may ask, "How are you doing?" But they're only trying to begin a conversation so they can talk about themselves. I talked with a guy who did that to me. As soon as I started answering his question and talked about my life, his eyes glazed over until I turned the conversation back to him and his most recent accomplishments. He didn't care about me at all.

Some parents live vicariously through the accomplishments of their kids. When their children are successful and popular, they're on top of the world, but when their kids struggle, they feel personally violated. Their identity is wrapped up in their kids doing well. To extend their brand as "good parents," they shamelessly talk about their kids' successes to everyone within earshot.

Fishing for Compliments

Due to our feeling of insecurity and our craving for affection, some of us say the exact opposite of what we desperately want to hear. Our self-degrading statements are bait for compliments. A girl tells her boyfriend, "Nobody loves me." She expects him to immediately respond, "But I do!" If he hesitates more than a nanosecond, he's in big trouble!

We hear people say things like, "I look horrible in this dress," "I can't do anything right," "I'm a rotten mother," "I'm a terrible cook," or "I'll never learn this skill." Our immediate desire for approval shapes a self-defeating statement or question with the hope that the listener will tell us what we long to hear. We're that desperate for affirmation, and we want it right now!

When people say these things to me, I've learned to avoid taking the bait. I just look at them and say nothing, or if I want to respond, I repeat their statement, "So, you feel horrible, and you can't do anything right." Usually, they feel caught: Gotcha! Then they quickly reverse course, "Oh, I don't know why I said that. I'll make it work." Or if a woman says, "I look terrible in this dress" and I agree, she instantly disagrees and defends her looks—which tells me she was fishing all along.

Instead of engaging in honest, meaningful dialogue about the condition of the heart, people who fish for compliments are taking a shortcut. It's a passive attempt to meet an active need.

Comparison

For years, I've prayed, "Lord, deliver me from the spirit of competition, the need to *be better than* and *have more than* someone else." Comparison is the fuel of our culture. We measure who we are and what we have against other people, all day, every day. When we're winning this game, we feel superior; when we're losing, we feel like pond scum. But success doesn't make us feel good for very long because we're afraid we'll lose our treasured position. Either pride or humiliation (or both) is a constant companion.

Most of us have only a few areas in which we're determined to win . . . or maybe only one. A beautiful woman doesn't care if she doesn't measure up in writing skills or designing buildings, but she pours over the magazines to see if there's someone else who might steal the praise she lives for. Musicians compare themselves with other musicians, salesmen with salesmen, golfers with golfers, and cooks with cooks. But these comparisons aren't trivial pursuits—our very lives depend on looking good in the eyes of others! Some people think that pastors should be immune to comparison, but we're human just like everyone else. At pastors' conferences, people jockey for position by talking about the size of their congregations and the immensity of their buildings. I've stopped talking about these things when I attend these events. I refuse to play this game any longer.

Though there are many similarities between men and women in their use of comparison to stake out an identity, men tend to focus on accomplishments and titles while women compare the quality of relationships, the groups in which they're accepted, and other intangibles of happiness and satisfaction.

Comparison poisons relationships. If our motive is to be one-up, we're always looking for an edge, a way to beat people instead of loving and supporting them. In everything we say and do, there are strings attached and hidden agendas. And of course, if our eyes are on beating others, pleasing God isn't even on the radar. No matter how well we perform and how many accolades we receive, we're always insecure because it's never enough to fill the yawning emptiness in our hearts and provide a stable, secure foundation of true love and acceptance.

> Comparison poisons relationships. If our motive is to be one-up, we're always looking for an edge, a way to beat people instead of loving and supporting them.

Is all competition bad? No. One form of competition can be productive. Competing with ourselves is a healthy alternative that provides a channel for our energy and creativity. When we love God with all our hearts and want to please Him, we can push ourselves to do more and be better—not because we're trying to prove we're worthy, but because we're thrilled that Jesus has already counted us worthy. We enjoy a healthy sense of satisfaction when we strive to do our best and make real progress, as long as we're competing with ourselves and not others.

FACING CRITICISM

People who live for approval are obsessed with what others think of them, and they're willing to change anything to please people. They're especially vulnerable to critics. I know. I've had my share of critics over the years. When I get an email or a letter or when someone tells me I need to improve in a certain area, I want to listen carefully to understand what they—and the Spirit—are saying to me. I have a lot to learn, and God uses correction from all sources to give me input, but I have to be careful to avoid knee-jerk reactions. In recent years, I've been told a lot of things that are humorous. (At least, that's the way I want to think about them.) If I let these strings of disapproval jerk me around, I'd be a basket case. Out of the long list I've compiled, I've picked forty. (I'm not putting any names next to them, so don't worry if you're one of the people who said one of these to me.)

"You drive a BMW."

"You drive a Mercedes."

"You drive a Porsche." (Actually, this one is true. Elton and Peggy Kirkpatrick heard me talking about always wanting a Porsche. They bought me a toy. I drive it around my office when kids come to visit. But actually, I drive a Ford pick up.)

"You fly a helicopter everywhere you go." (Seriously, in hilly Little Rock? Where would it land?)

"You buy all your shirts at Dillard's."

"We sing too many old songs."

"We don't sing enough old songs."

"We sing too many new songs."

"We need to sing more new songs."

"You dress up too much."

"You don't dress up enough."

"Pastors shouldn't wear jeans."

"Pastors shouldn't wear pink."

"You shouldn't go swimming."

"You spend too much time around students."

"You spend too much time around children."

"You spend too much time around lost people."

"You spend too much time studying."

"You don't hold up the Bible often enough when you preach."

"You use the wrong version of the Bible."

"You don't talk about politics enough."

"You talk about politics too much."

"You're a Democrat."

"You're a Republican."

"You keep your politics a secret."

"You don't preach enough on the end times."

"You don't shout enough."

"You talk about money too much."

"You should talk about money more."

"You need to preach more about faith."

"You need to preach more about grace."

"You should preach more about prophecy."

"You don't talk enough about sin."

"You don't talk enough about salvation."

"You need to talk more about Hell."

"You need to talk more about Heaven."

"You tell too many stories about your family."

"You should tell more personal stories."

"You should talk more about sex."

"You should never use the word 'sex' in the pulpit."

"You're too skinny to be a pastor. You need to gain weight." (A woman actually said this to me right after I became a pastor.)

"Marshmallow cream isn't any good on ice cream." (It's one of the few rules we have at our church. If we have ice cream, there has to be marshmallow cream. Why? Because I love marshmallow cream!)

Can you imagine what would happen if I tried to make all those people happy? I'd drive myself crazy! I'd be running around like a madman, trying to do everything for everyone all the time, but pleasing no one. I've only been a pastor for about a decade, and I've made a lot of mistakes. One of my biggest mistakes is the way I answered a lot of those people. Over and over again, I tried to explain why I did this or didn't do that. This strategy seldom worked, but I've learned my lesson. My answer now is this: If the criticism has any validity, I accept what God is saying to me, and

I pray, "Lord, I want to please You. What do You want me to do about this?"

I tried pleasing people. It didn't work. I want to please God. I'm going to make this my goal.

THE DARK SIDE

When we live as puppets on a string, we invite many problems into our lives. There are enough difficulties when we're walking closely with God. We sure don't need to multiply those by putting people in God's rightful place in our hearts! Let's look at the dark side of living to please people:

1. You allow people to easily manipulate you when they can prey on your insecurity.

The easiest way to control someone who wants approval is to use the potent power of disapproval. We learn this when we're very young. A toddler knows she can control her parents by withholding affection. In fact, the child instinctively knows she can get anything from her parents for the price of a hug! We also see it in dating, in marriage, with friendships, at work, and in every other relationship. The message is simple and effective: "If you don't give me what I want, I'll withhold approval from you." Manipulators have outstanding radar; they sense the people who crave approval.

> The easiest way to control someone who wants approval is to use the potent power of disapproval.

In an article in *USA Today*, Sharon Jayson reports that the desire for affirmation is stronger in college and university students than any other desire or need. She notes, "Sex, booze or money just can't compare with the jolt young people get from a boost to their self-esteem, says a new study of college students that found the desire for praise trumped other desires or needs."[1] But college students aren't different from the rest of us—we live for approval, and we die without it. Our craving for affirmation sets us up to be easily manipulated by the threat of disapproval.

2. You can never please everyone, and when you try to please everyone, you end up pleasing no one.

When we live to please people, we bounce off of the demands and expectations of others with dizzying speed. We change our position on a topic to make one person happy, but our new position alienates someone else.

3. You sacrifice standards in order to gain acceptance.

To close the deal and win the promotion, people in business are tempted to bend their ethics. To keep a boyfriend, a teenager jumps into bed instead of saying "No." To impress a friend, a person exaggerates the truth so that good things look a little better and bad things look a little worse. Many people in 12-step groups say their spiral into addiction started when their quest for acceptance led them to give in to an invitation to use alcohol or drugs, have illicit sex, or compulsively gamble.

4. You lose the respect of others. They see you shift with the wind and believe you stand for nothing.

Politicians are labeled "flip-floppers" when they change positions once too often, but we're no different. Our vacillation— changing our position to please the person in front of us at the moment—causes us to lose the respect of others who are watching us change our minds.

5. You lose your sense of identity. You lose track of who you are. You're simply being whatever you need to be to gain approval in that moment.

Some people are so focused on reading the faces and voices of others that they lose track of their own desires. They've worn a mask to win acceptance, but they've worn it so long that it's become fused to their faces. In fact, they no longer even think of themselves apart from their mask. Others are so insecure and indecisive that they don't even know what they want. I've heard someone ask, "What kind of pizza do you like?" But the person couldn't even offer an opinion. He just shrugged and mumbled, "I don't know. Whatever you want is fine with me."

6. You lose track of what really matters. God gets lost in the shuffle as you move from activity to activity that will please others.

When we live to please others, we play a continual game of Whack-a-Mole. We rush to say the right words and do the right things to win the approval of this person, but then we have to jump to please the next person who walks by, and the next and the next. It's a never-ending game—except that it's not really a game at all. It's a lifestyle that drives us insane. Where is God in all this? If we think of Him at all, we wonder why He isn't helping us be more successful at winning friends, being successful, and earning acceptance.

7. The goal continually shifts. What works today may not work tomorrow. Trying to keep up makes you tired because you have to remember what the latest brand is, what will impress people, and even who you're trying to impress. You feel you need to continually upgrade your life.

When we think we've finally got people where we want them, their mood changes, their desires shift, or they move to another city. No matter how well we've earned applause today, there's nothing certain about tomorrow.

We live in an upgrade culture. What was so cool yesterday is old hat today. Analog used to be in, but not any longer. The motto of the culture is "Bigger is better." A 42-inch screen may look big until we go over to a friend's house, but his 60-inch television looks so much better!

But it's not just stuff that we feel the need to upgrade. We also upgrade our friends. A person who got us into a group last month now seems so boring. Now that we're in, we realize another clique has even more prestige. Now, we set our sights on them. Upgrading relationships doesn't happen only in high school. Who are the people at work and church who we want to be seen with? Who are the "undesirables" who we'd rather not hang out with because being seen with them might make us look like losers?

People-pleasers live with a powerful blend of hope and fear. They've won a smile or an affirmation enough times to hook them into playing the game again and again. Even when they fail, they still have hope that next time, they'll earn a pat on the back or a hug. But they live in fear that they'll lose the prestige at work or the love they long for at home. This combination of hope and fear is tremendously manipulative. It cements them into a lifestyle of pleasing people at all costs—until and unless something breaks in to change the game forever.

NO UPGRADES NECESSARY

Those who are driven to please people simply won't change until a greater love replaces their previous desires. The love of Christ is the only power in the universe that can change a human heart, and with Him, there's no upgrade necessary. In the middle of Paul's letter to the Ephesians, he breaks into a spontaneous prayer about the incredible love of Christ. He prays,

> *My response is to get down on my knees before the Father, this magnificent Father who parcels out all heaven and earth. I ask him to strengthen you by his Spirit—not a brute strength but a glorious inner strength—that Christ will live in you as you open the door and invite him in. And I ask him that with both feet planted firmly on love, you'll be able to take in with all followers of Jesus the extravagant dimensions of Christ's love. Reach out and experience the breadth! Test its length! Plumb the depths! Rise to the heights! Live full lives, full in the fullness of God (Ephesians 3:14-19 Message).*

Those who are driven to please people simply won't change until a greater love replaces their previous desires.

Paul was as tough as nails, but God's love melted his heart. His prayer is beautiful and powerful. He asked the Father of heaven to unleash His power to change the hearts of his readers. He wanted God to convince them of the immeasurable width, length, height, and depth of His love—an experience of His compassion, kindness, tenderness, and commitment that far surpasses anything we can describe with words. Christ's love is far more satisfying than self-promotion, compliments, and comparisons. Are we looking for approval? It's here in full measure! Are we looking for love? There's no greater love in the universe? Do we want to be overwhelmed with God's kindness? It's so vast and deep that words can't describe it.

But Paul isn't finished yet. He concludes his prayer:

God can do anything, you know—far more than you could ever imagine or guess or request in your wildest dreams! He does it not by pushing us around but by working within us, his Spirit deeply and gently within us.

Glory to God in the church!

Glory to God in the Messiah, in Jesus!

Glory down all the generations!

Glory through all millennia! Oh, yes! (verses 20-21 Message)

God's dream for you and me is far bigger and grander than our highest dreams for ourselves. And He can pull it off! Like many people, I have a big imagination, but Paul knew that our wildest dreams would be easy for God to accomplish—if we'll trust Him and if we'll live to please Him above all else.

Wonder is an essential element of faith, but it's missing from the thoughts and prayers of many of us today. We're amazed at the advances in technology and medicine, but we take Jesus for granted. But if we want to live a life that pleases God, the first step isn't to reorder our schedules—we first need to reorder our hearts. Many people study the incredible immensity of the created universe and marvel at hundreds of billions of galaxies and distances measured in light-years. But I focus on the other end of wonder: It's amazing to me that the God who created everything knows and loves me personally. He knows my every thought, counts the hairs on my head, and is never surprised by anything at all. Some people are in awe of the grandeur of God; I'm amazed at the details God personally oversees in each of our lives every moment of each day.

When we live to please people, we lose ourselves, we lose the respect of the people around us, and we drift away from God. But when our affections are set on knowing, loving, and following Him, we experience more of His love than we can ever imagine. It's our choice every day. Which will you choose?

CONSIDER THIS . . .

1. What are some ways families encourage a child to please people above all else? How is this normal? When does it become harmful?

2. Paul indicates that there's no middle ground between pleasing people and pleasing God. Do you agree or disagree with his assertion? Explain your answer.

3. What does self-promotion look like? What harm does it do?

4. What is the motive underneath fishing for compliments?

5. How does comparison entice us to keep measuring ourselves others' standards? How does it poison our hearts and our relationships?

6. Review the "dark side" of pleasing people. Which one of these seems most painful and destructive to you? What damage does it do?

7. How is wonder an essential element of faith? What happens when we have it? What happens when we don't?

8. On a scale of 0 (not at all) to 10 (completely), how much are you experiencing the love of Christ Paul described in his prayer for the Ephesian Christians? What, if anything, needs to change?

3

WHO'S CLAPPING?

I have been crucified with Christ and I no longer live, but Christ

lives in me. The life I now live in the body, I live by faith in the

Son of God, who loved me and gave himself for me. I do not

set aside the grace of God, for if righteousness could be gained

through the law, Christ died for nothing!

A few years ago, I flew to the Philippines to meet with church leaders. While I was there, I met a lady who had been a high-ranking official in the government. She was smart and savvy. She had navigated through the labyrinth of her nation's politics to reach the top echelon of power. One day as she rode in her chauffeured limousine, she passed an enormous garbage dump. She noticed dozens of people picking through the trash to find discarded plastic bags they could bundle and sell for a few pennies. It was their only means of making a living. She had seen them and heard stories about them many times in the past, but on this day, the Spirit of God gave her compassion, and the sight broke her heart. She wept as she watched them, and she vowed to do something to help them. She didn't just feel sorry for the people picking garbage; she changed her life to meet their needs. To the dismay of other powerbrokers in her political party, she resigned from her position and started a little church—no more than a shack—in the middle of the dump.

Jay Martin is a successful attorney in Little Rock. Elected as a state representative, he was selected as the majority leader for his party. He was upwardly mobile in state government, his profession, and his finances, but he sensed God had more—much more—for him. He began serving as a lay pastor in an impoverished, gang-infested, crime-ridden part of our city. It's called Ives Walk. God gave him a deep love for the people he saw there. They had no hope, and they knew nothing of the transforming grace of God. Jay decided to do something about the crying needs he saw, but he didn't want to oversee another failed government program. Instead, he started small. One Saturday, he took a basketball out to a city court in Ives Walk, and he began bouncing it by himself. As a white guy in a black neighborhood, he looked out of place, but that didn't matter to him. After an hour or so, one kid came out to bounce the ball and shoot a few baskets with him. The next Saturday, the boy's two brothers joined them. Soon, Jay built a relationship with these three young men based on trust and respect. Today, Jay holds a church service every Thursday night for people our culture considers expendable. Homeless people and drug addicts sense there's something different about this guy. He doesn't speak *at* them; he talks *with* them. He cares, and they feel it. If you ask Jay what's most important in his life, he doesn't point to political power, financial wealth, or comfort. He points to the people God has put in his life, but they have come into his world only because he loves the applause of God more than the approval of man.

I know a couple who got their identity from the success of their teenage kids. The mother pushed her daughter to be a cheerleader and run for class president. She wanted her daughter to be supremely popular. "It'll be good for her," she told her friends as she made campaign ads for the election. And the dad lived vicariously through his son's football and baseball success. The kid appreciated the help, but he thought it was odd that sports were all his father wanted to talk about. The dad spent a small fortune on private coaches, summer clinics, and traveling teams so his son could be the best. When he did well, his dad's chest swelled with pride, but when he made errors on the field, his father chewed him out or blamed his coaches.

For years, a good friend of theirs tried to gently provide a mirror to show the couple how they had become obsessed with their kids' success, but they laughed it off. They didn't see that the pressure they were putting on their kids was causing their malleable children to be driven to win and easily discouraged by failure, and it was ruining their relationships in the family, too. Smothering parents may mean well, but they create deep insecurities in their kids because the message is clear: "You can't make your own choices. I have to make them for you."

Finally, the daughter's failed bid for office and the son's miserable baseball season caused enough pain that the parents had to be honest about their priorities. They realized they were furious at their kids for failing, and there was something about their anger that simply wasn't right. They talked to their honest friend, who again held up a mirror, but this time they saw the truth. It was a devastating, but transforming conversation. The parents realized they had been pressuring their kids—not for the son and daughter's sakes, but for their own prestige in the community. And they realized it was a spiritual problem: They had been trying to overcome their deep insecurities by their kids' success. Their friend pointed them back to Jesus, and they determined to please Him instead of being driven to win the approval of the people around them.

These parents had a long, tearful talk with their kids, and they promised they'd change. "We'll support you in whatever you want to do with your lives," they explained. "But we're through with our demands and smothering." The kids were very skeptical at first, but as the parents' repentance proved real, the son and daughter became convinced their parents had genuinely turned a corner. Finally, they began to have real, honest, affirming relationships. When the kids struggled, the parents didn't jump in to fix them or blame others. And when they succeeded, mom and dad celebrated without any strings attached. The daughter told a friend, "I don't know what happened, but my mom and dad are different people now. They love and accept me for who I am. I don't feel pressured any more to become someone they want me to be." What a glorious thing for a child to say about her mom and dad—especially this mom and dad!

The mom told a friend, "I'd rather my daughter love and follow Jesus than be class president, be head cheerleader, or date the handsomest boy in her class." The dad chimed in, "Yeah, and it's a lot better for my son to love God with all his heart than excel in sports. One thing lasts; the other doesn't." The earth had shifted on its axis, and it was a beautiful thing to see.

UNTOUCHABLE TREASURE

What does it mean to live to please God above all else? How can we live for the smile of someone we can't even see? In his letter to the Romans, Paul says that we can know and love God as His dearly beloved children. We've received the Spirit of adoption, "and by him we cry, 'Abba, Father' " (Romans 8:15). In *The Applause of Heaven,* pastor and author Max Lucado describes the relationship this way:

> *Sacred delight is good news coming through the back door of your heart. It's what you'd always dreamed but never expected. It's the too-good-to-be-true coming true. It's having God as your pinch-hitter, your lawyer, your dad, your biggest fan, and your best friend. God on your side, in your heart, out in front, and protecting your back. It's hope where you least expected it: a flower in life's sidewalk.[1]*

The Scriptures talk over and over about the incredible reality of our relationship with God. We were outcasts, helpless and hopeless sinners with no hope to earn God's approval, but God didn't wait until we shaped up. He sent His Son to die in our place, to spring us from the prison of sin and hell. He didn't just set us free and let us go off to make it on our own. He welcomed us into His family and made us sons and daughters of the King! We belong to the One who loves us more than we can ever know and who paid the price we could never pay. But like the people

When we think about the Christian life, we drift back to rules to define it. It's so sad. Instead of loving God with all our hearts, loving our neighbor as ourselves, and living the adventure of following Jesus, we make lists of do's and don'ts.

in Galatia, many of us forget that we are God's children. When we think about the Christian life, we drift back to rules to define it. It's so sad. Instead of loving God with all our hearts, loving our neighbor as ourselves, and living the adventure of following Jesus, we make lists of do's and don'ts. Since our permissive culture has a lot more do's than don'ts, many Christians try to be different, so they have a lot more don'ts than do's.

I'm convinced that what pleases God is the same thing that pleases me in my relationship with my sons—it's the warmth, spontaneity, and loyalty of our relationship, not that they follow some arbitrary set of rules. Do I have some expectations about their obedience and loyalty? Of course, I do, but those expectations flow out of our relationship and find meaning in the context of our relationship. Our love, understanding, and joy are the central elements of how we relate, not a set of rules.

If we start with a list of rules, we quickly end up with self-promotion to feel good about ourselves, and we compete to look better than others. But if we start with a relationship, we want to fulfill God's expectations for completely different reasons. In a letter to the believers in Corinth, Paul told them, "So we make it our goal to please him, whether we are at home in the body or away from it" (2 Corinthians 5:9). The word translated "goal" is really ambition. It's a strong word, one that you wouldn't expect in the Bible. We usually think of ambition as a selfish, sinful trait, but its value depends on its object. If our ambition is selfish gain, it's wrong, but if it's to please God, it's the most noble motivation known to mankind! A child who's convinced he's loved naturally wants to please his parents. It's the way life works in families, and it's the way it works in the spiritual world. In both cases, the results are increased love and loyalty. Jesus explained, "Whoever has my commands and keeps them is the one who loves me. The one who loves me will be loved by my Father, and I too will love them and show myself to them" (John 14:21).

When we look at the life of Jesus, we see something very clearly: He delighted in people who wanted to be near Him and express love to Him, but the rule-keepers always felt distant and resentful. The Pharisees and Sadducees multiplied strict laws, and they used them to crush the spirits of the people who couldn't measure up. Jesus didn't just shake His head at them. He blasted them as "white washed tombs" and a "pit of vipers"! Who were the ones who saw His smile? The woman caught in adultery who was saved by His kindness, Zaccheus the tax gatherer who was despised by everyone who knew him but who climbed a tree to see Jesus, children, lepers, the lame, and sick.

My favorite scene is recorded in Luke's gospel. A Pharisee named Simon invited Jesus and His men to have dinner with him, but Simon's hospitality was limited. He didn't ask one of his servants to wash their feet or anoint their heads with oil, which were customs of the time. During dinner, a woman who had previously met Jesus crashed the party. She was a prostitute, and she undoubtedly knew she wasn't on Simon's guest list. She didn't care. She was overwhelmed with gratitude for Jesus' love and forgiveness. Luke tells us:

> *She came there with an alabaster jar of perfume. As she stood behind him at his feet weeping, she began to wet his feet with her tears. Then she wiped them with her hair, kissed them and poured perfume on them (Luke 7:37-38).*

She had given Jesus the honor Simon had refused Him when He came to the party. When Simon growled his disapproval, Jesus taught him a lesson. He pointed out that the woman had poured out her love for Him when Simon hadn't even been cordial. Then He told His host, "Therefore, I tell you, her many sins have been forgiven—as her great love has shown. But whoever has been forgiven little loves little" (verse 47).

Love for God doesn't come out of a vacuum. We love, John tells us, because He loved us first and gave His life for us (1 John 4:9-11). Our love for Him is simply a response to His kindness, grace, and acceptance. It begins, though, with the realization that we're flawed. We deserve nothing, but He has given us everything. Our sins earn condemnation, but He has forgiven us and adopted us as His children. That's what grace is all about.

> Our love for Him is simply a response to His kindness, grace, and acceptance. It begins, though, with the realization that we're flawed. We deserve nothing, but He has given us everything.

As Paul continued his letter to the Galatians, he explained that life is much more than rules. The law is God's standard. It shows us that we're deeply flawed and in need of a Savior. A real relationship with Christ is the Spirit's work from the inside out. He told them, "For through the law I died to the law so that I might live for God. I have been crucified with Christ and I no longer live, but Christ lives in me. The life I now live in the body, I live by faith in the Son of God, who loved me and gave himself for me" (Galatians 2:19-20). And just to be crystal clear, Paul concluded, "I do not set aside the grace of God, for if righteousness could be gained through the law, Christ died for nothing!" (verse 21) If we insist that following rules is what's most important, we don't need Jesus at all.

Love is far more powerful than rules. When my boys were little, they played a game to see which one could get to me first to give me a hug when I came home. Every day, they came running out of the house to the car to be the first one. One day, Tyler called to ask how many minutes it would take me to get to the house. I told him I was about 10 minutes away. He whispered, "When you're in the neighborhood, call me." He wanted to be ready. I can imagine the disciples playing a game like that with Jesus. Did they know He was the Creator of the universe with all power and authority? You bet. When He calmed the storm on the lake that day and saved their hides, they were sure He was God in the flesh. Did they know He loved them? John called himself "the disciple Jesus loved." Does that mean Jesus only loved John and not the others? Of course not. But John was so overcome with Jesus' affection for him that it became the way he identified himself. Nothing else mattered. My boys' hugs and John's label for himself are more pleasing to me and to Jesus than any accomplishment or rigid rule keeping. We come to God with empty hands and open hearts. Love trumps all.

Lupita is a lady who serves at our church. One day she shared in our staff meeting that she was spending time working on an insurance claim. Later in the meeting, I asked her what was going on. I didn't know if a car got bumped in the parking lot or something else had happened at the church. She explained that it was a personal matter. Someone had broken into her home and stolen the computer and her jewelry. She told me that her husband's parents visit them every year and bring gold jewelry from Mexico. From the look on her face, I could tell that the loss of the rings and earrings was troubling her. "It's not the metal," she explained. "It's the memories." The look on her face, however, told me she had a very strong sense of God's peace. She told me, "They took things of value, but our real treasure—our love for each other—is untouchable." That's true in our relationship with God, too. We may be rich or poor in the world's eyes, but when we know Jesus, He's our greatest treasure.

HOW DO WE CHANGE?

If you've read this far in the book, you have a genuine longing to know and love God with all your heart. If the Spirit wasn't stirring you, you'd have put the book on the shelf before now. Let me give you a few principles about how God changes lives.

1. Realize change is necessary.

The first step in changing an attitude or pattern of behavior is the stark—and often uncomfortable—realization that what we've been doing isn't working. Many of us have been trying very hard to follow the rules, but instead of experiencing peace, joy, and purpose, we feel oppressed by guilt that we aren't measuring up. We wonder, *Is this the abundant life? If it is, I want out!* We may not know where to turn, but we're ready to get the help we need. Desperation never feels comfortable, but complacency never produces change—go with desperation.

2. Base your life on God's standard of truth: the gospel of Christ.

We might get a few good tips from Oprah or Dr. Phil, but they fall a bit short of being the authority on all of life as does the Creator, Sustainer, and Savior of the world! How do we know what God is like? By pouring over the Scriptures to discover His character. How do we know what it means to have a real relationship with Him? By looking at how He connected with people—from the Garden of Eden through the whole Bible. We find out the most about God by examining the life of Jesus. He is God in the flesh, and His relationships with all kinds of people show us how He wants to relate to us. What did He consistently communicate? Jesus told people of every stripe that there are two ways to be lost: by being very bad and by trying to prove you're good by following rules. The gospel cuts through to the heart by showing that no matter how sinful we are, Christ's love and forgiveness are far bigger. No matter how many

> No matter how many commands and rules we follow, they're never enough to fill the hole created by our sins. Only the gospel of grace meets our deepest needs and hopes.

commands and rules we follow, they're never enough to fill the hole created by our sins. Only the gospel of grace meets our deepest needs and hopes.

3. Opt out of upgrades.

If we're not careful, we can easily get caught up in the rat race of our society, whose theme song is "More, More! Faster, Faster! Bigger, Bigger! Better, Better!" If we buy into this system, we'll never be satisfied with what we have. We'll live with unfulfilled demands and resent the fact that others have what we want. Instead, opt out of our culture's penchant for upgrading everything. Learn to value simplicity, love, and purpose instead of filling your day with busyness. Spend less; give more. Worry less; love more.

4. Ask yourself, "Who's clapping for me?"

When we choose to please God above all else, some people will cheer, but others will think we've lost our minds. They just don't get it, and they feel very awkward around us because our values have changed. When others turn up their noses at our new choice to please God, it's a turning point: Will we go back to our old habits to avoid losing a friend, or will we keep moving forward to know, love, and honor Christ? Many people simply won't understand when we stop promoting ourselves, fishing for compliments, and playing the comparison game. But some of them—at least a few—will want what we've found, and we have the unspeakable privilege of pointing them to Jesus. When we get off the treadmill of pleasing people, we gain a wonderful sense of peace and security. We don't have to look over our shoulders all the time to see if someone is frowning at us or beating us at our game. We delight in

God's love, and we are glad when others succeed because our new security isn't threatened.

Ultimately, the thing that thrills our souls is the fact that the Creator of the universe delights in us, and when we respond to His love by loving Him in return, I can imagine Him raising His arms in heaven and yelling, "Wow, he gets it! I'm so glad!" Jesus said that when we live for Him, someday, we'll hear God's affirmation, "Well done, good and faithful servant. Come and share your master's happiness!" (Matthew 25:21) But I believe we don't have to wait that long. Every day—even today—we can sense His smile as we delight in His grace and live to please Him.

> Every day—even today—we can sense His smile as we delight in His grace and live to please Him.

What happens when we make daily choices to please God instead of living for the approval of others? A lot! We sense the presence and delight of God. Every child who is loved by his parents feels the parents' love. On a couple of occasions, the Father spoke out of heaven to Jesus so that everyone could hear. At His baptism, the Father announced, "This is my Son, whom I love; with him I am well pleased" (Matthew 4:17). Could it be remotely possible that Almighty God feels the same way about you and me? Yes, that's the incredible message of the gospel. We had been His enemies, but now, we are His children, the delight of His heart and the source of His pleasure.

The commitment to please God changes all of our human relationships. In his letter to the Romans, Paul said, "Love must be sincere" (Romans 12:9). What is Paul talking about? Since Adam and Eve, people have blamed each other and manipulated each other for their own gain. It's human nature, but it's not the nature of a child of God. As we increasingly experience the height and depth and width and length of God's love for us, our hearts are radicalized. We begin to love the people around us—and not just the nice people who like us. We begin to love even those who annoy us and those who want to hurt us. We can only love our enemies, like Jesus loved the Pharisees and died for them, too, if our hearts have been melted and molded by the matchless love of Jesus.

As we become less defensive and less manipulative, and as we open our hearts to the difficult people in our lives, something amazing happens. Solomon, who was the wisest man of his age, remarked, "When a man's ways are pleasing to the Lord, he makes even his enemies live at peace with him" (Proverbs 16:7). For some of us, our minds are consumed with thoughts about our enemies. We relive conversations and events over and over, experiencing the hurt multiple times, and daydream about getting even. Or maybe we're trying to figure out a way to say just the right thing the next time to control the angry person's behavior. We may devise widely varied strategies to control people: We yell and cuss, cry and feel sorry for ourselves, or make demands and accusations. Whatever we're trying to do, our attempt to control others ruins our lives! But when we focus on pleasing the Lord, we can relax more, stop controlling others, and love them with no strings attached. As we'll see later in the book, loving them sometimes means we speak words of correction, but still, we don't demand a response.

When people sense that we aren't demanding and controlling any longer, they stop being as angry and defensive with us. That's what Solomon was talking about. When we live to please God, we not only please Him, we eventually gain the respect of men. When we live our lives to please men, we lose their respect and harm our relationship with God. When we see it this way, it's an easy choice, isn't it? A quick analysis of the consequences shows us: "Of course, I want to please God! That's such a better option. I don't want the applause of men; I want the applause of heaven."

Actually, Paul wrote that it's a good and noble thing to please people, but with a different motive in mind. He explained, "Each of us should please his neighbor for his good, to build him up" (Romans 15:2). Is he contradicting what he wrote to the Galatians? Not at all. When we're pleasing people to win their approval because we're insecure, it's all about us. Our kindness, compliance, and hard work to "serve" them are manipulative, not loving. But when we genuinely love and please Christ, we want to help others, not control them for our gain. Our goal is to build them up, not win accolades for ourselves.

Sadly, many churches teach that love is a strategy to build a better marriage, better friendships, or better parents. But the love of God is much more than a strategy we use to accomplish a limited goal. It's the overflow of God's presence from the heart of a believer who is captivated by the grace of God. It's not a strategy; it's life, and it permeates every choice, every relationship, every thought, and every goal. Outside of God's grace transforming our hearts, our motives in relationships are always suspicious. Only a genuine experience of God's love, at a level that "surpasses knowledge," provides the freedom and desire to love people with no strings attached.

JESUS' WARNING

Probably the most famous parable Jesus told is the one we call "the prodigal son," but it's actually a story about two brothers and their relationship with their father. You know the story: The younger son asks his dad for his share of his inheritance (while the dad is still alive!), runs away, and blows it all on "wild living." When he loses everything, he takes a big step in career advancement by feeding pigs for a foreigner. In Jewish culture, that was the lowest anyone could go. But one day, he "came to his senses." He has hit rock bottom and is determined to go back to his father's house to ask for a job as a day laborer. When his father sees him coming home, the old man runs down the road, hugs and kisses his son, and interrupts the young man's confession to shower him with love and restore his status as a cherished son. It's a great story, but that's not the point Jesus was making. There's another brother. This guy has done everything right. He has stayed with his father, worked hard on the farm, and obeyed every command. When he hears that his dad has restored his little brother, he's furious! His dad is throwing a party for his brother, but when his dad comes out to the field to invite him to celebrate with him, the older brother refuses to join them.

To understand the impact of this story, we have to look back at Jesus' audience. Luke tells us, "Now the tax collectors and sinners were all gathering around to hear Jesus. But the Pharisees and the teachers of the law muttered, 'This man welcomes sinners and eats with them'" (Luke 15:1-2). The story depicts the two groups of people listening to Jesus that day. The younger brother represents the "sinners"—the misfits and outcasts, the prostitutes, tax collectors, thieves, lame, and blind. Jesus' message for them was clear: No matter who you are or what you've done, come to your senses and come home to God. His open arms of grace await you! But the older brother in the parable represents the grumbling, mumbling Pharisees and religious teachers, the ones who have followed every law to the letter and have despised Jesus for loving the misfits. What's the message to them? "The Father loves you immensely. You've been doing right things, but you've been doing them for wrong reasons. Your hearts are hard, but it's not too late. Lay aside your self-righteousness and resentment and come to the feast to celebrate. The party is for anyone who is willing to accept God's grace!"

The story ends with the dad standing in the field, inviting the angry, older brother to the party. Only one son enjoyed the father's love and attended his celebration. Do you think the Pharisees standing around Jesus got the point of the story? You bet they did! At that point, Jesus probably gazed into the eyes of the scorning religious elite with a look of kindness. He desperately wanted them to accept His offer of love. How deep was Jesus' love for these hardhearted leaders? He graciously told them about God's open invitation, but He knew that only a short time later, these same men would call for His execution.

The parable, then, is a wonderful invitation and a stern warning. To those who are humble enough to admit their flaws and are eager to come home, the Father eagerly waits to embrace them.

But those who insist on making rules the measuring stick of their lives remain outside the celebration—feeling superior, but resentful, bitter, and alone.

This is exactly the point Paul was making in his letter to the Galatians. The invitation and warning are written in every line. "Come back home to God's grace," Paul tells them with kindness. "But if you refuse, you'll miss out on the joy, love, peace, and thrill of the Father's celebration. It's your choice."

TWO MOTIVES

As we think about living wholeheartedly for God, we quickly become painfully aware that we fall short—way short. How do we respond when the Spirit shows us that we don't love God with all our hearts, we've been manipulating people instead of loving them, and we've put success, pleasure, and approval in the center of our lives? In one of his letters to the Corinthians, Paul explains that there are two kinds of repentance: "godly sorrow" and "worldly sorrow." In his first letter, he had said some hard things to them. They had been committing sexual sins, dividing into competing factions in the church, arguing about virtually everything, gossiping, and drifting away from God. (Sound familiar? People haven't changed much in the last two thousand years.) When Paul got word that the people had taken his message to heart and repented, he explained the two very different responses. He said, "Godly sorrow leads to salvation and leaves no regret, but worldly sorrow brings death" (2 Corinthians 7:10).

When we, like the Galatians, think that rules are the most important part of our spiritual lives, we hate to be told we're flawed in any way! Our self-concept and security are wrapped up in being right, so we fiercely avoid any suggestion from anyone that we may be wrong. We only feel good about ourselves if we're meeting the standards, so any suggestion we fall short results in acting defensive ("I didn't do that!"), blaming others ("It's her fault!), excusing ("I couldn't help it."), or minimizing ("Oh, it wasn't that bad.). None of these responses result in the cleansing of forgiveness

> When we long to please God, we're glad for Him to show us where we're off base. Instead of hating ourselves and blaming others for our flaws, we draw close to God, delight in His forgiveness, and commit ourselves again to honor Him in all we do.

and the joy of knowing God's smile. We either beat ourselves up, we beat others up, or we try to act like nothing's wrong. All of these "worldly sorrows" produce new layers of guilt, resentment, and denial, which deaden us spiritually and alienate the people around us.

But the other kind of sorrow is very different. When we long to please God, we're glad for Him to show us where we're off base. Instead of hating ourselves and blaming others for our flaws, we draw close to God, delight in His forgiveness, and commit ourselves again to honor Him in all we do. In fact, we're so eager to please Him that we don't even wait for the Spirit to tap us on the shoulder to show us our faults. Like David, we pray:

> *Search me, God, and know my heart;*
> *test me and know my anxious thoughts.*

See if there is any offensive way in me,

and lead me in the way everlasting (Psalm 139:23-24).

Rules or relationship—the way we view the Christian life determines how we respond to God's correction. When Jesus corrected the rules-loving Pharisees, they killed Him. When He corrected the people with humble hearts, they loved Him even more.

Many years ago, a pastor who wanted to help his people live by the grace of God often asked a simple but profound question: "Right now, are you a child of God?" If people answered, "Well, I'm trying," he knew they were still trusting in their ability to meet certain standards to earn God's approval. But those who got it, those who really understood the grace of God, responded with wide-eyed wonder, "Yes, isn't it amazing? God loves me and accepts me because of His grace, not because I've done anything to deserve it. And I'm so thankful!" So, how would you respond to this question? Are you still trying to measure up and feeling guilty because you don't (or maybe feeling prideful because you have a long list of boxes you're able to check off)? Or have you given up on self-effort and turned to the One who has paid the price for you? If you have, you're full of wonder and gratitude. There's nothing like grace to change a person's heart.

> We can't exalt Jesus while we're promoting ourselves.

10 QUESTIONS

We can't exalt Jesus while we're promoting ourselves. Every morning, I pray, "Lord, help me to give you all the credit for any success. Not me, Lord, but You deserve all the praise." I also ask, "God, put a catch in my spirit if I'm about to say or do anything that puts me on Your pedestal. Let me see it before it happens. I don't want to be the center of attention. I want You to receive all the credit."

I've developed 10 questions to help us analyze our motives. Reflect on these for a few weeks until they become ingrained in your mind and heart:

1. Do I get angry when I don't get all the credit I think I deserve?

2. Do I try to promote myself, my ideas, and my contributions? Is my goal to be known and respected?

3. How do I respond when someone else is honored? Am I happy or jealous?

4. Do I feel compelled to remind others of my importance?

5. What's really more important to me: getting credit for myself or having God receive glory? Is this commitment reflected in my responses to people and situations?

6. In conversations, do I remind others about my past victories when they're sharing a success?

7. Do I gladly affirm others with the hope they'll praise me in return?

8. When my contributions aren't given equal billing, how do I respond?

9. Am I competitive with others about kingdom things?

10. How do I react when something makes me look like a failure or when I perceive my image has suffered?

A person who is concerned about his own glory is obsessed with his reputation instead of pleasing God. I challenge you to live by a different code. Drop out of the "race to impress" and live for His glory, not yours. You'll discover how freeing it is!

SOME PRACTICAL ADVICE

So . . . how does a person change from seeking the favor of people as a first priority to living for the applause of God? Each of us faces countless points of decision, and the accumulation of good choices creates a new habit of living only and always for God's approval. Let's look at a few choices we face:

When you feel the rush of being applauded at work, at home, in sports, in church, or anywhere else, it's intoxicating! There's nothing wrong with enjoying affirmation—unless it becomes our ultimate good that defines us. When you get a pat on the back, enjoy it, but thank God that His approval is far more valuable and far less fickle.

When you feel the sting of criticism, have the courage and integrity to ask, "Is it true?" and "What part of it is true?" Admit the hurt, avoid retaliation, take responsibility for any wrongs or flaws, and choose to rejoice in God's deep and unconditional love.

When you serve tirelessly, but nobody seems to notice, it's easy to become resentful. We don't mind being a servant as long as we aren't treated like one! Many of us labor tirelessly at our work, take care of endless responsibilities at home, and care for others in our lives, like neighbors or our parents. It hurts when nobody seems to care. We need to remember that Jesus served people day after day—and ultimately gave His life—for thankless people. When we continue to faithfully serve without recognition, we're becoming a little more like Him.

When your mind is flooded with the fear of a person's disapproval and the hope of being praised, step back and recognize the destructive, oppressive force of these thoughts. Refocus your attention on the gospel of grace and remember that you are more valuable to God than the stars in the sky. You belong to Him!

As we take steps to change how we think, feel, and act, we shouldn't be surprised when we realize we've failed—again. Take heart. Like a parent who is thrilled with a child's effort and love even when it's flawed, God is thrilled with our attempts to please Him. Let the truth of His Word penetrate your heart and permeate your thoughts. Three passages provide some direction.

The writer to the Hebrews told us:

Therefore, since we are surrounded by such a great cloud of witnesses, let us throw off everything that hinders and the sin that so easily entangles. And let us run with perseverance the race marked out for us, fixing our eyes on Jesus, the pioneer and perfecter of faith. For the joy set before him he endured the cross, scorning its shame, and sat down at the right hand of the throne of God. Consider him who endured such opposition from sinners, so that you will not grow weary and lose heart (Hebrews 12:1-3).

Rivet your focus on Jesus, not the people around you.

In a second passage, Peter reminded us what Jesus suffered:

When they hurled their insults at him, he did not retaliate; when he suffered, he made no threats. Instead, he entrusted himself to him who judges justly (1 Peter 2:23).

When we face ridicule and rejection, we have an example to follow.

And in a third passage of Scripture, Paul wrote the worried people in Philippi:

Rejoice in the Lord always. I will say it again: Rejoice! Let your gentleness be evident to all. The Lord is near. Do not be anxious about anything, but in every situation, by prayer and petition, with thanksgiving, present your requests to God. And the peace of God, which transcends all understanding, will guard your hearts and your minds in Christ Jesus (Philippians 4:4-7).

Paul tells us that in good times and bad, we can choose to rejoice in God's love, pray like crazy, and thank Him for His answers even before they come.

Read these passages, think about them, make them your prayers, and watch how God uses them to point out wrong thoughts and replace them with new desires to please Him. It won't happen by magic, and it won't happen overnight, but gradually, you'll see genuine change in your deepest desires. It's a beautiful thing!

BEYOND CIRCUMSTANCES

If our goal is to please people, we can never be sure we're measuring up. We began the pursuit to win approval out of insecurity, so every smile or frown we see on people's faces makes us feel even more unsure of our status. But when our ultimate aim is to please God with all our hearts, we

> In fact, it's the one purpose in life that's immune to outside influences—we can live to please God through the good times and bad.

aren't destroyed by disapproval or shaken by difficult circumstances. In fact, it's the one purpose in life that's immune to outside influences—we can live to please God through the good times and bad. I believe we please God most when the chips are down and our faith is threatened. It's easy to sing praises when everything is going right, but clinging to Jesus when our lives are coming apart pleases Him immeasurably. I can picture Him like the manager of a prizefighter. When the boxer comes back to the corner after getting beaten to a pulp in a round, the manager washes him off, gives him a drink, and says, "Don't give up. You can do it. Hang in there, kid!"

Some church leaders promote the false expectation that walking with God guarantees an easy life. They claim that if you give enough, come to church enough, and follow enough rules, God is obligated to bless you. They say that God wants you to have your best life now. That's not consistent with Scripture. Every true believer, from Abraham and Joseph to Jesus and Paul, endured suffering when they chose to follow the Father's will. Jesus told His followers, "In this world you will have trouble" (John 16:33). That's not a promise many people want to claim! But it's a fact of life for every person on the planet, even for believers who want to please God. As we grow stronger in our love for God, He tests us—not to make us fail, but to make us stronger. If we misinterpret the tests as our failure or God's abandonment, we'll run from God instead of to Him. Don't make that mistake. During a time of real hardship, my good friend Alton Garrison told me, "Anyone can pilot a ship in a calm harbor, but we were meant to captain the ship in the storm."

A few years ago, Dave Richards was walking with God and enjoying his family. When he didn't feel well for an extended period, he went to the doctor. Tests showed he had kidney cancer. He endured rounds of surgery, radiation, and chemotherapy. He suffered physically, but he and his family also suffered emotionally because they didn't know what the outcome might be. During all this time, Dave didn't blame God. His faith grew stronger as he trusted God's goodness and greatness even in this difficult dark time in his life. Dave had always been a kind person, but the testing of cancer deepened his love for God so that the kindness of Jesus overflowed from him more than ever. Dave learned he could please God in the light, but maybe even more in dark times.

The children of Israel needed reminders of God's deliverance from Egypt, so Joshua told them to put piles of stones in the Jordan River after they crossed into the Promised Land. I need a reminder, too. Years ago, I put a note on my desk that said simply, "Is God clapping for me right now?" This simple question arrests my thoughts, challenges my motives, and reminds me that His smile is the only thing worth living for.

Will you put a sticky note on your desk or a card in your wallet or purse with that question? I dare you to try it. God may use it to turn your life upside down and inside out—in a very positive way.

CONSIDER THIS . . .

1. How does seeing Christ as an "untouchable treasure" change our values, motivations, and relationships?

2. What are some things that have to happen in a person's heart in order to even want to please God?

3. What does it mean to "opt out of our culture's upgrades"? Who do you know who is choosing God and simplicity over busyness and stuff? Is this lifestyle attractive to you? Why or why not?

4. What are some ways pleasing God purifies our relationships so our love for people is sincere and not manipulative?

5. Describe the two kinds of sorrow. Which of these have you experienced most often when the Spirit corrects you? How would your life be different if you had more "godly sorrow"?

6. What are some ways suffering can purify our motives to please God?

7. Have you put the question, "Is God clapping for me now?" on your desk or in your pocket? How do you think it can help you?

4

RUNNING ON EMPTY

Question #2:

Are you so foolish? After beginning by means of the Spirit, are

you now trying to finish by means of the flesh?

Not long ago, I bought a car that has a dashboard monitor of the number of miles left in a tank of gas. I'm pretty analytical, so I love gauges. My friend, Steve, and I were driving from Dallas to Little Rock, and we knew we were about to enter a long stretch of highway with no gas stations. The gauge showed that we could go 50 miles before we would run out of gas. The next gas station was 30 miles away. No problem. When we got to the exit, the monitor showed we could go another 20 miles. Why get off too soon? Steve pressed on the pedal, and we went on down the road. After about five miles, the gauge didn't show 15 miles to go. It read a double asterisk. I didn't know what that meant, but I was pretty sure it wasn't good news. We talked about what to do, and Steve's solution was to speed up to 90! I had the audacity to question his logic, and he solemnly told me, "Rod, if we're going this fast, we can coast a lot farther if we run out of gas."

At that speed, the next 15 miles came and went in a flash. When we saw the exit, I think we were both leaning forward. (Body English is very effective in those situations.) When Steve parked in front of the pump, we each let out a big sigh of relief. The tank held sixteen gallons, and it took exactly sixteen gallons to fill it up. We'd been running on fumes. When we realized how close we had come to walking to get gas, we said to each other, "Man, that was so stupid!" We instantly realized we would have wasted a lot of time if we'd run out of gas on the highway. We had been running on empty, trying to see how far we could go without any fuel in the tank.

Far too often, the drive with Steve is a metaphor for our lives. We're running on empty, but we speed up to see how far we can go when we're completely out of spiritual fuel. Many of us live on empty all day, every day.

SNAPSHOTS OF EMPTINESS

Bethany had been very successful in her new business—until the recession hit. After months of desperately trying to keep it afloat, the red ink got the best of her, and she finally gave up. She told me dejectedly, "I don't know why God let this happen. Why me? Why now? I'm not sure I can ever trust Him again."

Phil and Marsha had tried very hard to raise their three kids to have good values and feel loved. Two of them are grown and walking with the Lord, but their youngest became a prodigal.

Sarah had always had a mind of her own. When she was a teenager, she pushed the limits as far as she could. And when she went to college, she found friends who made her teen rebellion look tame. Marsha blamed herself: "These things don't just happen," she sobbed. "It must be my fault . . . all my fault."

But Phil blamed God. He stopped attending church, and his relationship with Marsha and the kids became strained. Instead of turning to God, he turned away from Him. When Sarah was in high school, Phil had tried to control her behavior, but he had failed miserably. When he put the clamps on her, she pulled away even more. "I should have handled it a lot better," he remembers. But he still blames God for letting it all happen.

John was a regular at church for years, and he served faithfully in several different ministries. He was always very meticulous about being on time and doing everything he was assigned to do—in fact, he always did more than anyone expected. He was smiling on the outside, but his worship and service were devoid of joy. His friend, Bill, had enough insight to talk to John about his perfectionism and rule keeping, but John wasn't willing to listen. He dismissed Bill's attempts to talk about grace, freedom, and joy. "I know what God expects of me," John insisted. "And I'm not going to fail." After a few years, the crushing weight of guilt drove John into a deep depression. He's still there.

When we think the Christian life is a bunch of rules, our solution is to gut it out, grit our teeth, and obey, or we give up completely because it's so hard with so few rewards. Some people who have tried to live by rules have crashed and burned, emotionally, relationally, and spiritually. At some point, they realized this way of living just doesn't work. A catastrophe, a broken relationship, a shattered dream, an addiction, or depression ran them off the rails. But others are still trying—and they're trying really hard. Like the Pharisees and the Judaizers, they still think that following enough rules, hard enough and long enough, will be good enough to make them feel okay about themselves. For those who have given up, this chapter is a breath of fresh air; for the ones who are still trying to gut it out, it's a wake-up call. All of us need to learn to live by the grace and power of the Spirit. Like the Galatians, we all started our walk with God with a sense of joy and gratitude for His forgiveness, but somewhere along the way, our spiritual gas tank began to run dry. If we haven't learned to continually fill it up, we run on fumes, then on empty—and sometimes we crash and burn.

At the beginning of our Christian walk, we were very aware of our failures and needs. We prayed, "Lord, I need You," "Father, give me wisdom to make this decision," "Jesus, if You don't come

> Like the Galatians, we all started our walk with God with a sense of joy and gratitude for His forgiveness, but somewhere along the way, our spiritual gas tank began to run dry.

through, I'm sunk," "God, I need You to use me in my friend's life. I can't do it alone. I need Your power to change her life," or "Lord, I don't know what to do. Will You help me?" As we depended on God, He did wonderful things in us and through us. It was amazing! We saw Him work in our marriages and families, our careers, our friendships, and every other part of our lives. As time went by and we saw all these blessings unfold, we started thinking, "I must be a pretty cool Christian for God to bless me like this!" And our eyes shifted from God's grace and power to our talent and success. When we began, we focused on God's power, God's wisdom, and God's love, but we drifted toward trusting in our plans, our abilities, and our intelligence to make life work. We then concluded, "God, you're sure lucky to have me on your team." This switch is deadly. The phrase I sometimes hear among Christians—even leaders in the church—is that "I'm a self-made man." This statement is at the height of arrogance and self-sufficiency. In reality, everything we have, everything we are, and every talent we possess are gifts from the hand of God. A few years ago a wealthy businessman told me he was a self-made man. I responded, "That's great. Why don't you make another one?" I don't think he was amused, but he got the message.

For most of us, the experience of daily dependence on God sometimes comes very slowly, but thank God, it comes. One of my friends owns a business, and for years, he experienced great success. When the economy turned south, however, his business struggled. One day, when we talked about trusting God in the middle of difficulties, he told me, "Success—it's all because of God. The more you begin to think it is yours, God lets you have all the responsibility and pressure. I prayed my business into being, but I forgot to pray it into growing."

Paul wrote the Corinthians about an important spiritual principle, one that we seem to forget over time. He remembered a prayer he prayed for God's deliverance, as well as God's answer of "No."

> *But he said to me, "My grace is sufficient for you, for my power is made perfect in weakness." Therefore I will boast all the more gladly about my weaknesses, so that Christ's power may rest on me. That is why, for Christ's sake, I delight in weaknesses, in insults, in hardships, in persecutions, in difficulties. For when I am weak, then I am strong (2 Corinthians 12:9-10).*

The Galatians had forgotten this principle. Many of us forget it, too. As we spend time in the faith, we might think that we will grow more dependent on God, but strangely, over time, many people become more dependent on rituals and rules. The richness of knowing and loving God is gradually replaced by a dead bunch of do's and don'ts. It's a shame, but it doesn't have to happen this way.

Grace is counterintuitive.

GRACE, FIRST AND ALWAYS

Grace is counterintuitive. Human nature screams for us to be self-sufficient, to depend only on our ability to make life work, to please the people in front of us, and to forget our Creator and Savior. Many of us drift away from God after we've begun well. How does this happen? For some, success breeds complacency and the misplaced expectation that God will always enable us to go higher and higher with no problems at all. But others walk away from dependence on God because they're convinced He's let them down. Disease, death, divorce, and discouragement cloud their minds and cause their hearts to grow cold. When difficulties come, they conclude, "God's plan isn't working, so I'd better devise my own plan." But we can never accomplish God's purposes through our own strength and wisdom. Some of us become so discouraged that we abandon God's plan altogether.

Our culture certainly supports our tendency to trust our own wisdom and power instead of trusting God. At one point, I typed "personal power" in Google, and I got over 47,000,000 hits. Every site tells us how to be bigger, better, stronger, and more efficient than our peers. We live in an incredibly competitive society, and we admire people who have "made it." We want to be just like them, so we buy their books and watch their DVDs to learn their secrets. If you walk into any bookstore, you'll find shelf after shelf of self-help books. The writers give instructions on everything imaginable, from surviving a bear attack to cooking French cuisine. There's nothing wrong with learning new things, but there's something very wrong with leaving God out of the classroom. For Christians, the lure is subtle. We read books and go to conferences to find the magic bullet to ensure that our business or church will grow, to become great leaders or parents, or to get help to overcome some deficiency in our lives. Certainly, we want to grow and learn, but what and who are we depending on: the techniques taught by people or the power of the Spirit?

I'm an advocate of using the tools at our disposal, but I'm afraid that the incredible resources at our fingertips can numb our sense of dependence on God. It's a lot easier to search the web for an article to tell us how to handle a problem than to open the Bible and pray for God to give us wisdom. Our church has had the privilege of helping plant hundreds of churches around the world. I have found the most radical dependence on God in the most desperate conditions. I visited a pastor who started a church in Tanzania. He built a simple stick and grass thatched building for the church, but the radical Muslims in the community burned it to the ground. We were able to provide the funds for him to build a metal building. The Muslims pulled this church down, too, but this pastor wouldn't give up. In spite of fierce opposition and threats to his life, he trusted God to change lives. I have a picture of him speaking to his congregation as they sit on wooden benches next to the ruins of the church. When opposition increased, his faith grew even more, and God is using him to touch dozens of lives.

The long history of God's people is that they often became complacent and self-sufficient when they experienced God's blessings. They drifted away from Him, so God brought suffering into their lives—disease, invasion, captivity, drought, and famine—to show them they couldn't make it without depending on Him. I'm convinced that we don't have to go through cycles of blessing and suffering—if we have the wisdom to trust God first. Of course, our trust in Him doesn't make us immune to the problems of having a fallen nature and living with fallen people in a fallen world. There will always be trouble in our lives, but if we learn to depend on God, the trouble won't be God's hand of correction. We'll at least eliminate *that* cause from the reasons we experience hardship.

The Galatians had been going to church, and if there had been conferences, they would have attended those, too. They had a long checklist of things they were doing to prove they were worthy of God's acceptance. They studied and worked hard, but it was all self-effort. Paul wasn't going to put up with their drift. He told them bluntly:

> *You foolish Galatians! Who has bewitched you? Before your very eyes Jesus Christ was clearly portrayed as crucified. I would like to learn just one thing from you: Did you receive the Spirit by observing the law, or by believing what you heard? Are you so foolish? After beginning with the Spirit, are you now trying to attain your goal by human effort? (Galatians 3:1–3)*

Paul took them back to Square 1—the cross of Christ. Before he called them fools for trusting in their ability to keep all the laws as the way to prove themselves worthy to God, he told them, "I do not set aside the grace of God, for if righteousness could be gained through the law, Christ died for nothing!" (Galatians 2:21) When I studied this passage, I wrote in my journal: "I never want to set aside the grace of God!" Grace is the antidote for empty, rigid self-righteousness.

The word "fools" is a very strong word. It's not like calling your friend a "knucklehead" or another term that's half joking. There was nothing funny in Paul's language! He was criticizing them in the strongest terms for abandoning their only hope and going back to the empty rituals and oppressive rules they had turned from when Paul was with them. This is like an alcoholic who has been sober for years and restored his family relationships but "goes back out" into his addiction. It's like a woman who has left a life of prostitution and created a wonderful, loving family but walks out on them to return to her life of paid sex and false intimacy. It's like a prodigal who has gone home, mended his relationship with his parents and siblings, and joined the family business but chooses to walk away from it all to go back to "a far country" of wild living and shame. How did Paul respond? Just like the wife of the alcoholic, the husband of the prostitute, and the parents of the prodigal—he was brokenhearted, and he spoke hard words with the sincere hope of turning them around. If I see someone on the streets of Little Rock who is messing up his life, I may pray for him. But if one of my sons was throwing his life away, the love in my heart would explode in determined action! I'd grab him by the shoulders, look him in the eye, and say, "Son, you're being a fool! Don't you see how you're messing up your life? Come back, son. Come back. I'll help you in any way I can." Paul's deep love prompted his fierce words to the Galatian people.

The Galatians were trusting in themselves because that's the only resource for people who insist on living by rules.

The Galatians were trusting in themselves because that's the only resource for people who insist on living by rules. They had forgotten the beauty and the power of the gospel of grace, so they failed to tap into the Spirit's power to equip them to live the

Christian life. Human effort simply can't match the wonder and power of God's Spirit. They were running on empty. God had given them a car with a powerful engine, but they were pushing it down the road. The sad thing is that they were proud of the progress they were making! But it was nothing compared to the surge of power God wanted them to experience—if they'd only trusted in Him.

Why do we depend on ourselves instead of God? There may be many different reasons for different people. Some of us are impatient with God's timing. We want Him to show up and change things now! Some of us think we know what needs to happen better than God knows. We're sure we've figured out how God should work, but we're not sure He got the memo. We've decided to take things into our own hands. And some of us don't want to trust God because we realize He'll get the credit. If we live for applause, we sure don't want to share it with anyone else—even God.

TWO ERRORS

Christians in Paul's day and in ours often make one of two errors in understanding spiritual life. We see it as either *magical* or *mechanical,* and sometimes a blend of both. I've talked to people who were sure that if they prayed the right prayer, God was obligated to give them what they wanted. If the blessing didn't appear, they condemned themselves for not having the right technique, or they blamed demons for their troubles. Our connection with God isn't like rubbing a genie's bottle and getting instant results! We relate to Him as our loving and wise, but mysterious Father whose eternal plans are far above anything we finite humans can imagine.

Others go in the opposite direction. Like the Galatians, they've reduced the Christian life to rules, rituals, and disciplines. They experience very little joy and wonder. Their lives are a constant grind, and they can never be sure they've done enough. They've identified lots of hoops they think they have to jump through, and they feel rotten if they fail to get to all of them. They read a book that offers a formula for spiritual power, and they try it for a while. When it doesn't work, they buy another book, and another and another. They're always looking for "the secret" that can make their lives perfect, full of blessings and devoid of problems.

And some of us are so creative that we do both. We're rigidly dedicated to particular rituals and habits to prove that we're good Christians, but we also secretly hope that we can find just the right prayer or "new truth" that will lift the burden of guilt off our shoulders.

Many of us have signed up for promises Jesus never made. We use the magical or mechanical means to ensure that our lives will be pleasant, our children will be obedient, our jobs will be meaningful, and we'll have plenty of money to enjoy life. But if we're to "become like Jesus," we'll face the same hardships He faced, and we'll be thrilled to see the Father use us like He used Jesus. Some popular books and speakers promise an effortless life—if we just follow their formula for success. That's baloney. A life of faith always includes both crosses and crowns. Our expectations may need some radical restructuring.

The call to follow Jesus inevitably involves a measure of suffering and leaving some valued things behind. The church in America has forgotten the simplicity and power of Christ's invitation to follow Him by denying our selfish desires and taking up our cross. The people who heard Jesus in the first century understood very well that his reference to the cross wasn't about gold jewelry and the top of steeples. He was telling them to willingly lay down their comforts and reputation and take up an electric chair of self-denial. Human nature wants to cling to the best of both worlds, the spiritual and the natural, but Jesus will have none of it. He calls us to lay down our lives for Him, but only in response to Him first laying His down for us. The only true fulfillment is in abandoning our old thirsts and drinking deeply of the love and purposes of God, but this choice always comes at a price. Jesus didn't promise His disciples an easy life. He asked them to leave behind their comfort, prestige, and resources, but He promised the life they'd find in Him would be well worth the cost. The Christian life isn't a helicopter ride to the top of the mountain. It's a long hike with a trusted friend. Along the way, we expend plenty of effort, but we are carried along by the beautiful views around each bend and the joy of being with someone who loves us.

> The only true fulfillment is in abandoning our old thirsts and drinking deeply of the love and purposes of God, but this choice always comes at a price.

THE COVER UP

The Christian life is a paradox. The way to be filled is to admit we're empty. The way to have real joy is to have a broken and contrite heart. The way to experience glory is to become a servant of all. We are strong only when we are honest about our weakness. We experience God's love and forgiveness as we come to Him with our most tragic flaws. But people who are wedded to laws and are trying to prove they're worthy by keeping commands can't afford to be honest about their faults. They hide them as much as humanly possible! We think we're so smart to engage in a grand cover up. We may be able to fool some of the people, some of the time, but eventually, people find out—and we can never fool God. He knows everything. What are some motivations to be honest?

Hiding our flaws doesn't work.

People aren't stupid. They have eyes, and they notice what we say and do. Trying to camouflage weaknesses doesn't work for a marriage, a friendship, or a church. You don't have to have a Ph. D. in psychology to see beneath the surface. You may see someone who is loud and abrasive, always has an opinion about everything, and has to be the center of every conversation. If you have a success, he takes credit for it. He wants everyone to know how smart, special, and wonderful he is. What is going on in this person's heart? What's he trying to hide? He's attempting to compensate for gnawing feelings of insecurity, but it's a pitiful, pathetic attempt, and observant people see right through it.

And of course, even if we're successful in hiding our faults from people, God sees everything in laser-sharp clarity. If we want to please Him, we increasingly realize that we're in His presence all day, every day. That truth sounds threatening to someone who is trying to hide, but it's a comfort to those who want to honor the One who loves them.

When you hide a weakness, it remains a problem.

If we won't admit a flaw, we'll never improve. People in 12 Step programs understand this principle better than most. In Step 1, "We admit we are powerless over our addiction, and our lives have become unmanageable." There are countless addicts in our culture, but only those who admit they're flawed and needy take steps toward recovery. The principle, though, isn't just for addicts. It applies to every flaw of every person on the planet.

> If we won't admit a flaw, we'll never improve.

Occasionally, a parent or spouse calls my office to make an appointment for someone he cares about. Often, the person being referred to me is an addict. I always ask, "Why isn't he making the appointment?"

The answer is usually, "He doesn't believe he has a problem."

If that's the case, he's not ready to receive any help I—or anyone else—can give him.

This principle is true across the board. I can't help you with your marriage until you first admit there is a weakness, a conflict, or a problem.

You won't lose weight until you admit you've gained too many pounds.

If you're a gossip and people avoid you, you'll never stop spreading secrets until you admit you have a heart problem of insecurity.

If you won't face your financial problems, the debt won't magically go away; it'll get worse.

At this point, some readers may be thinking, *I like this idea of admitting faults. The solution is to get my spouse to admit to all those faults. Then things will be better!* Sorry, but that's not how it works. You have to admit *your* weaknesses and flaws and work to remedy them. Get the log out of your own eye first. Maybe later, God will use you to take the speck out of another person's eye.

At our church, I often tell our team, "A leader is always working on a weakness. I should be able to ask you, 'What are you working on?' and you should have an instant answer. You shouldn't have to think about it even for a moment." One key to getting better—as a leader, a parent, a husband, an employee, an athlete, or in any other role—is to identify and work on weaknesses.

Do we only work on weakness? No. Another component to improvement is to find a way to maximize our strengths. Become a student of your talents, and work hard to use your God-given abilities.

The matchless love of Jesus and the awesome power of the Spirit are available to any believer all day, every day, but there's a prerequisite: We have to admit we're flawed and weak so that the boulder of pride is taken out of the channel and the life of Christ can flow freely into us and through us. As long as we try to hide our faults from God and people, we short circuit God's mighty power to transform lives, including our own.

FILLED UP

Being filled with the Holy Spirit isn't some strange electrical charge that makes us light up. The term is synonymous with Paul's other explanations of spiritual life, such as "knowing the love of Christ that surpasses knowledge." It's all about the relationship. To develop any meaningful relationship, we have to make some effort to spend time with the person to find out more, ask questions, and build trust. It's the same with God. We

> Living *for* God without spending time *with* God is like trying to use a cell phone without recharging it at night.

can't know the love that passes understanding by giving God an hour a week or a few minutes each day. If we really want to know Him, we have to invest in the relationship. Good intentions aren't enough. Living *for* God without spending time *with* God is like trying to use a cell phone without recharging it at night. It might last two days or even a little more, but eventually, you find yourself staring at a useless piece of plastic and metal that's disconnected from the world. God is our source. To experience His love, forgiveness, and strength, we have to stay connected to our source.

God is attracted to empty people. He can't fill people who are full of something else. He longs to fill those who admit their tanks have run dry. Jesus said, "Blessed are those who hunger and thirst for righteousness, for they will be filled" (Matthew 5:6). He's not impressed with how many people we impress by keeping so many rules. He looks past all that into our hearts. Are we hungry for Him? Do we thirst for His presence and power? Do we delight in the remarkable truth that we who were destined for hell have been rescued by Christ's death, a payment that bought us and made us God's children? Life has a way of puncturing holes in our spiritual tanks, so we leak. That's not an indictment; it's just a fact. Unless we're constantly being filled with the Spirit, we soon become dry. Too many Christians are running on empty. They're focused on their own reputations, and they try to use God to help them become more impressive. That just doesn't work in God's kingdom. The prophet, Hanani, told the king of Judah, "For the eyes of the LORD range throughout the earth to strengthen those whose hearts are fully committed to him" (2 Chronicles 16:9). God is still looking. Has He found you?

CONSIDER THIS . . .

1.   Describe what it means for a person to be "running on empty."

2.   Read Galatians 2:19 through 3:5. How would you paraphrase Paul's message to the people?

3. What are some ways people think of spiritual life as magical? How do they treat it mechanically? What are some results of both of these errors?

4. Why do many people try to hide their flaws? What are some results of trying to hide them from God?

5. What is the connection between God's grace and our sense of purpose? How does depending on our ability to follow the rules shape our sense of purpose? Which is more attractive to you? Why?

6.   What are some things you're doing to deepen your relationship with God so that you genuinely experience His love, presence, and power? What are some ways you might need to change your priorities and schedule to make more time to pursue God?

7.   What do you think it means to be filled with the Spirit? Is this your experience at this point in your life? Explain your answer.

5

OUR PART, GOD'S PART

Because you are his sons, God sent the Spirit of his Son into our

hearts, the Spirit who calls out, "*Abba*, Father." So you are no

longer a slave, but God's child; and since you are his child, God

has made you also an heir.

Sometimes, God goes to great lengths to show us how much we need to depend on Him. A few years ago, I was the speaker at a kids' camp. Actually, it was a one-man show. I led worship, taught, and did anything else that had to be done. I was feeling pretty good about being God's choice servant. On Wednesday night that week, my voice vanished. I tried to speak, but only a whisper came out. There was no second string speaker to step in for me. I was it, and I was as silent as a rock. How in the world could I speak to these kids? When I thought things couldn't get any worse, they did. The air conditioner broke, so we had to move to the cafeteria. I don't know if you remember the acoustics of cafeterias, but they sound like the inside of a jet engine at full throttle. I got up and motioned that I was a bit handicapped. Then

I started to lead the kids in worship. The last song was "Amazing Grace." As we sang, something amazing happened. People began weeping. Kids were filled with the Holy Spirit. Children spontaneously prayed for adults, and adults knelt to pray for children. It was one of the most powerful, life-changing services I've ever seen, but I quickly realized my part in it was nil. They hadn't responded to my insightful, eloquent speaking. My inspiring song leading hadn't moved them. They had responded to the Spirit of God totally apart from my talents.

I went back to my room, lay on my bed, and cried. The Lord whispered to my heart, "Rod, I love you, but I don't need you. In My grace, I choose to use you, but I can change lives without your help. When I work, it's not about your abilities—it's about My power unleashed in you. Don't forget that." I made a promise to God that night that I'd never try to serve Him again in my own strength. I woke up the next morning with a restored voice and a healed heart.

Times of suffering and setbacks aren't the end of the world unless we interpret them as God withdrawing His favor from us. That night at the kids' camp, I'm convinced God orchestrated me losing my voice so that I could learn one of the biggest lessons of my life. There may be many reasons we face tough times. Certainly, we might suffer as a consequence of sin, but God also leads us into darkness so that we learn to appreciate the light. Times of trouble give us a different perspective. We realize that seeing God use us is the highest privilege life can offer. He chooses to use flawed people like us to accomplish His magnificent purposes to redeem men and women, boys and girls from sin and death. He owes us nothing, but He gives us everything.

PARTNERS

In his letter to the Philippians, Paul gives us a brief theological treatise about the nature of spiritual life. In two verses, he captures the essence of his teaching in all his letters to the churches. After he described the sacrifice of Christ in three movements—stepping out of heaven, dying for our sins, and exalted in heaven—he wrote:

> *Therefore, my dear friends, as you have always obeyed—not only in my presence, but now much more in my absence—continue to work out your salvation with fear and trembling, for it is God who works in you to will and to act in order to fulfill his good purpose (Philippians 2:12-13).*

In our walk with God, we're not passive, expecting Him to magically do things to change us and use us. We're active partners in the process. But make no mistake: We're *junior* partners. In several letters and in a couple of places in his letter to the Galatians, Paul makes it clear that we've been adopted as sons and daughters of the King.

> We're active partners in the process. But make no mistake: We're *junior* partners.

One of the most amazing truths is that we who were outsiders have been made insiders. Now, we have the unspeakable honor to be part of the family business. What's God's business? It's redeeming the world, changing destinies, and bringing justice and love to a broken planet. As Paul told the Philippians, we labor, we sweat, and we take action, working out our salvation in fear and trembling. Notice: We aren't working *for* our salvation—that's self-justification, which is the opposite of the gospel of grace. We work because we're saved, we've been rescued, and we now follow in Jesus' footsteps and honor Him in all we do. Certainly, discipline is important, but we don't trust in our rituals and spiritual habits to earn points with God. We use them to deepen our relationship with Him. Spiritual disciplines (Bible study, prayer, service, worship, giving, confession, and so on) aren't all gritted teeth and determination. They are means to know, love, and serve God more fully.

As our hearts and lives are aligned with God, He works powerfully in us to accomplish His purposes. Do you see the connection between the first and second questions we've been studying? As our hearts change and we want to please God more, we want His purposes more than personal power, affluence, or approval. We begin to care about what He cares about, and we want what He wants. As this alignment happens, the Spirit is unleashed in us and through us to work powerfully to accomplish God's purpose of restoring families, redeeming souls, and bringing justice and love to a broken world.

GET IT RIGHT

How does Paul explain spiritual life to the law-loving Galatians? By using their own arguments against them. They had gone back to Old Testament laws to prove their righteousness and earn God's approval. Paul gives them three examples of why this approach is so foolish. First, he tells the story of Peter's drifting back to the law. Peter had opened the door of the gospel to the Gentiles when he led the Roman soldier, Cornelius, to Jesus, and the big fisherman enjoyed good fellowship with people the Jews had always despised. But when some Jews came to town, Peter became afraid of their condemnation, so he switched sides. Peter's actions proved to be a bad example to other Christians. Paul—never one to mince words—explained what he said to Peter:

> *When I saw that they were not acting in line with the truth of the gospel, I said to Cephas [Peter] in front of them all, "You are a Jew, yet you live like a Gentile and not like a Jew. How is it, then, that you force Gentiles to follow Jewish customs? . . . So we, too, have put our faith in Christ Jesus that we may be justified by faith in Christ and not by the works of the law, because by the works of the law no one will be justified" (Galatians 2:14, 16).*

Even Peter wasn't immune to correction. Round 1 went to grace over law.

The Jews revered Abraham as the father of their nation. The Judaizers pointed to him as the paragon of their belief that following the law would earn big points with God. Paul's second correction is to point out that the promise of salvation was given to Abraham *before* God gave him the law pertaining to circumcision—a practice that set the Jews apart from every other nation. Paul explained:

> *Understand, then, that those who have faith are children of Abraham. Scripture foresaw that God would justify the Gentiles by faith, and announced the gospel in advance to Abraham: "All nations will be blessed through you." So those who rely on faith are blessed along with Abraham, the man of faith (Galatians 3:7-9).*

Two down, one to go.

Paul continues to point out that the promise given to Abraham was based on faith, not law. All the laws of the Old Testament, he explains, were given to show us that we can't ever measure up, not to prove we can! They reveal the selfishness in our hearts so we'll turn to the One who is the ultimate fulfillment of the promise: Jesus Christ. The law isn't evil. It's holy and right and good, but it has a limited purpose—not to save us, but to point out our need for a Savior. Paul told them:

> All the laws of the Old Testament, he explains, were given to show us that we can't ever measure up, not to prove we can!

Is the law, therefore, opposed to the promises of God? Absolutely not! For if a law had been given that could impart life, then righteousness would certainly have come by the law. But Scripture has locked up everything under the control of sin, so that what was promised, being given through faith in Jesus Christ, might be given to those who believe (Galatians 3:21-22).

Three for three. Okay, Paul was telling the Galatians, if you want the law, I'll give you the law. It shows God's holiness, but it doesn't have the power to save. Only Jesus Christ, the fulfillment of the promises to Abraham, Moses, and the prophets can rescue us from the sins the law exposes in our lives. Paul concluded his tour through the Old Testament with a startling conclusion. The Jews had excluded Gentiles, women, children, the sick, the blind, the lame, and anyone else who didn't meet the strict criteria of being a Jewish male of a certain age who had followed all the laws. In stark contrast, Paul claimed that the gospel of Jesus is inclusive and magnificent:

> *So in Christ Jesus you are all children of God through faith, for all of you who were baptized into Christ have clothed yourselves with Christ. There is neither Jew nor Gentile, neither slave nor free, nor is there male and female, for you are all one in Christ Jesus. If you belong to Christ, then you are Abraham's seed, and heirs according to the promise (Galatians 3:26-29).*

Some people today might think, *All that stuff about Peter, Abraham, Sarah, Hagar, dietary laws, promises, and covenants is so antiquated. What does it have to do with me?* Good question. If we insist on using our ability to follow a set of rules and meet a standard to feel good about ourselves, we need to realize that this tactic has been tried before. It's not just a pretty good idea that isn't quite right—it's nuts! Jesus gave His life to free us from the bondage of guilt and shame because we can never measure up to God's standard of righteousness. If we think we can, we become like the Pharisees—arrogant, with a superiority complex, and hardhearted, but secretly insecure. The grace of Jesus breaks through our crusty exterior, melts our hearts with His love, and releases us into a radical freedom to live for Him. The message of the gospel is the worst news and the best news anyone has ever heard. It tells us that our best efforts aren't enough. We're hopelessly lost and without a shred of hope to fix things on our own. But Someone has done it for us. Jesus Christ stepped out of the glory of heaven to live the life we couldn't live and die in our place to pay the penalty we couldn't pay. When we get an inkling of that freedom and joy, we delight in God's love and experience the power of the Spirit.

THE BATTLE

A great preacher was once asked, "Sir, are you filled with the Spirit?"

He responded with a smile, "Yes, but I leak."

Spiritual life, like all relationships, isn't static. We have to keep investing in knowing, loving, and following Jesus, or our hearts grow cold. He has given us a stunning freedom: "It is for freedom that Christ has set us free. Stand firm, then, and do not let yourselves be burdened again by a yoke of slavery" (Galatians 5:1). Paul warned them against being "burdened again" by the guilt created by the law. It's a form of slavery. One of the saddest things I see is when people return to their own yoke of slavery, guilt, and shame. I know a young man who was a classic prodigal. He left home, got involved in sex and drugs, and found himself in jail for selling cocaine. After his release, he came to a wedding at our church, and we struck up a conversation. Over time, we kept talking on the phone and during his visits to our city. He was gloriously saved and freed from his former life. For three years, he walked with God and was a light to everyone around him. Then he went back to the town where he was arrested to visit a friend. For weeks, I didn't hear from him. Finally, his parents told me he had gone back to his previous lifestyle. People go back to a previous way of life because they remember the good times and are brain dead about all the heartaches they endured. Selective memory is a poor teacher. The dependence on rules to make our lives work is just as wrong as drug abuse. It's far more socially acceptable, but we have to remember that Jesus was very patient with the prostitutes, tax gatherers, and other misfits. The ones who incurred His anger were the rigid rule keepers. It's just as easy for legalistic people to revert to their old slavery of living by a checklist as it was for my young friend to go back to the drug culture. Paul pleaded with the Galatians, "Don't go back!" God is pleading with us, too.

To stay strong in grace, we have to fight against our sinful natures, the world's temptations and lies, and the devil's schemes. It's always easier to revert to rules or give up entirely on pleasing God. We fight the battle to stay strong in the grace of God every moment of every day. Undoubtedly, Paul had taught the Galatians this truth when he was with them years before. Now he reminded them:

> *So I say, walk by the Spirit, and you will not gratify the desires of the flesh. For the flesh desires what is contrary to the Spirit, and the Spirit what is contrary to the flesh. They are in conflict with each other, so that you are not to do whatever you want. But if you are led by the Spirit, you are not under the law (Galatians 5:16-18).*

Is that your experience? It certainly is mine. Even on my best days, I don't do the things I know I should do, and I do some things I know I shouldn't. If righteousness comes through doing everything right, I'm sunk! But as we experience the love, kindness, and power of God, basking in our relationship with Him and marveling at His grace, we'll have the desire and the power to say "No" to selfish desires. They won't go away until we see Jesus, but the Spirit's power will enable us to fight well.

To help the Galatians understand what he meant by "the desires of the sinful nature," Paul gives them a long list of vices. Paul points out sixteen behaviors and attitudes that dishonor God and ruin lives. They begin with sexual immorality and end with orgies. In between, he hammers on traits in every human heart: hatred, jealousy, fits of rage, and selfish ambition. We may laugh at these sins when we watch them portrayed on sit-coms, but Paul isn't amused. They're serious business.

Paul provides a stark contrast to these sinful traits by giving another list. This time, he tells us about the character qualities the Spirit produces in people who want to please God and trust in His power. We call these "the fruit of the Spirit": "love, joy, peace, patience, kindness, goodness, faithfulness, gentleness and self control." I can imagine Paul winking at them when he wrote the next line: "Against such things there is no law" (Galatians 5:22-23). No, there's no law against any of these traits! This transformation and overflow doesn't happen by following a list of rules, but only as a result of a dynamic, loving relationship with Christ.

> A synonym for spiritual vitality is to be "full of God."

Some people see this list of fruit as a checklist—another set of rules to follow. It's not that at all. A synonym for spiritual vitality is to be "full of God." If we focus our attention on Christ's grace and purposes, and if we delight in His love, we'll be filled with Him. He'll then gradually or spontaneously change our hard heart into a tender heart, he'll enable us to be kind to annoying people we previously tried to avoid, we'll become good listeners instead of demanding to be heard, and we'll celebrate when others succeed instead of being threatened. When we're full of God, His life courses through our veins.

What's overflowing from your life? "Out of the abundance of the heart the mouth speaks" (Luke 6:45). If an objective person watched you and me for a couple of days, what would he say fills our hearts to the point of overflowing? It's a tough but enlightening question.

Some of us think of Paul as a guy who was tough. He was, but he valued relationships. It's fascinating to me that in this letter of fierce correction, Paul explains that the power of the Spirit produces rich, meaningful relationships with God and with God's people. After he told the Galatians that Christ has set them free from the oppression of rules, he offered a summary comment: "For in Jesus Christ neither circumcision nor uncircumcision has any value. The only thing that counts is faith expressing itself through love" (Galatians 5:6). Faith isn't demonstrated by rigidly following a prescribed list of rules, but only by having the faith that connects us with the heart of God so that His love flows into us and out of us to others.

At the end of his description of the fight to be dependent on God instead of giving in to selfish desires, he warned:

> *Those who belong to Christ Jesus have crucified the sinful nature with its passions and desires. Since we live by the Spirit, let us keep in step with the Spirit. Let us not become conceited, provoking and envying each other (Galatians 5:24-26).*

How do we know the Spirit is powerfully at work in us? By the love we have for the people around us—especially those who used to get on our nerves!

BENCHMARK

We need daily reminders to shift from self-dependence to God-dependence. When our hope is in our efforts and our strength, we're in big trouble! But when our hearts are aligned with His, we want what He wants, we trust in His power, and we're thrilled for Him to get the credit He deserves. In Jesus' day, rabbis wrote prayers for their followers to pray. When His disciples asked Jesus for a prayer, He gave them one: the Lord's Prayer. Every morning, I use this prayer as a reminder of where my heart should be. It's become a benchmark for my motives and my dependence on God.

I pray, "Thine is the kingdom and the power." I often elaborate, "God, I need Your strength and power today. I need Your anointing on my life. My talents and abilities aren't enough to do what You want to accomplish, and the brilliance of the people around me won't cut it, either. I need You, Lord."

One Christian leader once sadly reflected, "I'm afraid I trust God as a last resort." I don't want to do that. I want to trust Him in the good times as well as the bad. This part of the prayer reminds me that I can't fulfill God's assignment by using only my resources. I need God in order to do anything significant. Jesus told His men, "Apart from me, you can do nothing" (John 15:5). I'm starting to really believe that!

Every morning, I use this prayer as a reminder of where my heart should be. It's become a benchmark for my motives and my dependence on God.

Then I pray, "For Thine is the kingdom, the power, and the glory forever." It's not about me working hard to build my kingdom and advance my reputation in our church, our city, and our denomination so that I'll get all the praise. Just the opposite. I want everything I say and do to point to Jesus Christ. There's a vital link between God's purposes and His power. If our purpose is to advance our reputation, God withholds His power. But if our deepest desire is to honor Him, He unleashes the forces of heaven and earth as resources at our disposal. His timing and methods may be different than we'd like, but we can count on Him to work in His way, in His time, and for His fame.

This part of the prayer often causes me to stop and take stock of the condition of my heart. Everything in our culture of power and prestige pulls us in the other direction. Everywhere we go, we see people jockey for position. They shamelessly promote themselves, climb the ladder, and build their personal brand. But I don't want to build my brand—I want to build Jesus' brand. I want Him to receive the applause He deserves. My choice each day is to live for my fame or His. I choose His.

We can't exalt Jesus while we're promoting ourselves. The two are mutually exclusive. Every morning, I pray, "God, I want You to use me today, but I promise to give You the credit for everything good that happens. Thank You for the incredible privilege of using me, but I realize You can do it all without me. Don't let me drift into self-promotion. If I climb onto the pedestal, cause Your Spirit to tap me on the shoulder and whisper, 'Watch out, Rod!' You deserve to be there, not me."

GRATITUDE

All we're saying about spiritual life leads us to one conclusion: It's all about God, not about us. When we realize this fundamental fact, God does some amazing things in our hearts. We become less demanding and more giving; we complain less and thank Him more. We develop that precious and elusive quality: humility. Humble people are the most thankful people on earth, and thankful people remain humble because the act of giving thanks is always other-focused. Gifts flow toward gratitude. Who do parents love to give things to? To their children who are delighted to receive them. In the same way, I believe God loves to shower His blessings on people with humble, thankful hearts. They receive His gifts gladly, praise Him for His generosity, and then pay it forward by giving more to others.

Let's be honest. Do we focus on all the things we want and how much we don't have? Are we bent out of shape because we believe life has given us a raw deal? Or do we look beyond the tangible and physical to focus on our spiritual blessings that will never change: the forgiveness, love, and presence of God? I know some sour people who find something wrong with a bowl of ice cream on a summer day, but I also have been with people who are grateful to God even in their darkest moments. Those are the people I want to hang around. Those are the ones I hope will shape my life. Gratitude is both a choice and a result. We can decide to thank God even when it looks like the bottom has dropped out of our situations. Thanking Him tells Him we're trusting in His purposes and provisions, and it reminds us to depend on Him. As we walk with God day after day and are filled with His Spirit, our hearts are gradually transformed. They become less sensitive to criticism but softer to sense God's touch. Through it all, we develop a deep, rich, overwhelming gratitude for God's kindness in our lives.

> Thanking Him tells Him we're trusting in His purposes and provisions, and it reminds us to depend on Him.

Keeping in step with the Spirit is a lot like water skiing. Try it without a boat. You won't get far, you won't have fun, and you'll look pretty stupid out there in the water by yourself. You can have the finest skis money can buy, a fancy swimsuit, and a world-class rope, but if you don't have a boat, you'll look like a fishing cork bobbing in the water. When you're connected to a powerful boat, amazing things can happen. You still have to develop some skills—like hanging on for dear life! But as long as you hang on and keep your balance, you'll go places and have a great time.

Life in the Spirit isn't asking God to bless our plans and efforts. It's first asking Him to show us His plans so we can align our hearts with His. Then, as we trust the power of His Spirit and we hang on, His strength pulls us along. And it's quite a ride!

CONSIDER THIS . . .

1. What does it mean to be a "junior partner" in our relationship with God?

2. Read Philippians 2:12-13. What's the blend of our part and God's part in a vibrant spiritual life? How does (or would) understanding it this way encourage and revitalize your walk with God?

3. What are some reasons it's important that our purposes are aligned with God's? How does our sense of purpose determine our experience of God's power?

4. What's the power source for people who insist on getting their identity from following rules?

5. Describe the freedom of living in grace? Does it set us free to do anything we want? Why or why not?

6. How would you explain the battle Paul talked about in 5:16-18? How do we fight this battle? What are some signs we're winning or losing?

7. How might praying the Lord's Prayer each day help you keep in step with the Spirit?

8. Who is the most grateful person you know? What's different about him or her? Is this attitude attractive to you? Why or why not?

9. What is your part and what is God's part in a vibrant spiritual life?

6

DO YOU REALLY CARE?

Question #3:

Have I now become your enemy by telling you the truth?

Philip was a freshman in high school when he trusted Christ as his Savior. His father was the mayor of a town near Little Rock, and Philip loved to hang out with our family. For several years, he was at our house at least once a week. His family had very little church background, so his dad sometimes slipped into the back of our worship services after they started, and he left before we finished so no one would notice him. He was very curious about the God his son had found.

Our family loved Philip. He became a third son to me and a brother to my boys. When he was a senior, he began dating a very pretty girl. In a short time, I saw that she wasn't a good influence on him. At first, I tried to casually engage him about their relationship, but he was defensive. Then I became more direct: I warned him about the girl he was dating and about the direction of his life. I pleaded, "Philip, I've seen this many times before. You were doing so well in the faith. You were becoming the man God wants you to be, but in the past several weeks, the Lord and His purposes have taken a backseat to your girlfriend. Please come back."

He said the right things to me in that conversation, but I knew his heart wasn't in it. In the next couple of weeks, he gradually withdrew from our family, the church, and, most tragically, from Christ. I called him and asked him to have lunch with me so we could talk about the drift that had become apparent to everyone who loved him, but he refused.

That was the last straw. He completely abandoned everything and everyone who had mattered so much to him. I tried to follow him for the next couple of years when he went to college. When social networking became possible, I tried to reconnect with Philip on Facebook. The message came back that my friend request had been denied. He had cut me completely out of his life. In the moments after I got that message, I went outside, sat on the curb, and wept. He knew I loved him so much I had to tell him what he didn't want to hear, but he now considered me to be his enemy—and it hurt.

Sometimes, telling others the truth isn't as traumatic and painful. Several years ago, our worship team had dinner together. We all ordered fried chicken, and in the middle of the dinner, one of the guys noticed that Ron had a piece of chicken stuck to his forehead—not just a tiny piece of crust, but a chunk of meat! The guy who noticed it kicked me under the table and nodded toward

Ron. I could barely control my laughter. When another member of the team looked at me like I'd lost my mind, I discreetly motioned to look at Ron's head. For about ten minutes, we laughed uproariously at anything Ron said. He thought he'd become the funniest comedian in the world. Finally, we told him the truth. He reached up and took the piece of chicken from his forehead, and we all had a good laugh again.

The last thing I do before I get up to preach is to check my zipper. I hope someone would love me enough to tell me if it was unzipped, but you never know. Some guys get upset when someone gives them this awkward information, but wouldn't you rather know than not know?

One day, I walked to my car in our parking lot, and I noticed three of our maintenance guys, Perry, Billy, and Jack, struggling to break into Perry's car. I yelled to ask what was going on, and Billy said, "He locked the keys in the car, and we're trying to unlock it. We've got a coat hanger, but it's taking a while." All three of them were taking turns trying to maneuver the crook of the hanger to the lock, but they weren't having any luck. I could tell they were getting frustrated. They considered calling the police to come to open the door for them. I walked over to the passenger side of the car, and I noticed the window was down. Without saying a word, I reached in, grabbed the keys, and tossed them to Perry. They had missed the truth of the situation. If they'd had a different angle on the problem, it would have been solved in a flash. (These guys love for me to tell this story about them, so don't worry that they'll feel exposed.)

DEFENSIVE AND DEFIANT

When Paul heard that the believers in Galatia had drifted away from the grace of Christ back to a system of rules and rituals to feel good about themselves and earn God's acceptance, he got all over them. His first question was about their motive: Who are we trying to please, God or people? The second question addresses the issue of power: Are we trying to change our lives by human effort or by the work of the Spirit? When we trust our talents, experiences, and smarts, we get into big trouble. Paul makes the connection between the problems they were experiencing and the God they were neglecting—and he invites his readers two thousand years later to make the same connection. He realizes the harshness of his letter. Like a loving parent correcting a disobedient and foolish child, he now looks not at theology but at his relationship with his readers. A parent may say, "Look, son. I'm telling you this for your own good. I'm not against you. I'm for you." In the same way, Paul asked them, "Have I now become your enemy by telling you the truth?" (Galatians 4:16)

> Paul makes the connection between the problems they were experiencing and the God they were neglecting

When Abraham Lincoln took the oath of office on March 4, 1861, several Southern states had already left the Union, and several more were on the brink. His inaugural address made it clear that he would defend the nation, but at the end, he pleaded with the people of the South to think again about their choices. His closing sentiments echo Paul's letter. Before he sat down, Lincoln proclaimed:

In your *hands, my dissatisfied fellow countrymen, and not in* mine, *is the momentous issue of civil war. The government will not assail* you. *You can have no conflict without being yourselves the aggressors.* You *have no oath registered in Heaven to destroy the government while* I *shall have the most solemn one to "preserve, protect, and defend it." . . . We are not enemies, but friends. We must not be enemies. Though passion may have strained, it must not break our bonds of affection. The mystic chords of memory, stretching from every battlefield, and patriot grave, to every living heart and hearthstone, all over this broad land, will yet swell the chorus of the Union, when again touched, as surely they will be, by the better angels of our nature.*[1]

Lincoln had spoken the truth with boldness and compassion, but the people of the South didn't respond as he had hoped. When we speak truth to the people we love, there are no guarantees. We prepare well, speak clearly, and let God work in their hearts—if they'll let Him.

Paul's question about the Galatians' response to his correction wasn't in a vacuum. For two paragraphs, he reminded them of his love, his untiring efforts, and the suffering he endured for their sake. First, he reminded them of their spiritual journey from pagan worship to know and love the true God:

Formerly, when you did not know God, you were slaves to those who by nature are not gods. But now that you know God—or rather are known by God—how is it that you are turning back to those weak and miserable principles? Do you

wish to be enslaved by them all over again? . . . I fear for you,
that somehow I have wasted my efforts on you (Galatians 4:8,
9, 11).

Then Paul gets personal. He tells them to think back on his time with them. He had been sick with an eye disease, but they didn't reject him. Instead, they welcomed him warmly and generously. When he told them about Jesus, they gladly embraced the gospel and found new life. They appreciated Paul so much that he says they would have ripped out their eyes and given them to him. Of course, he was exaggerating, but it was an important point: The Galatian believers dearly loved Paul. Now, as they read his stinging letter of correction, he was afraid they would see him as an enemy because they didn't want to hear his message. He wrote them:

As you know, it was because of an illness that I first preached
the gospel to you. Even though my illness was a trial to you,
you did not treat me with contempt or scorn. Instead, you wel-
comed me as if I were an angel of God, as if I were Christ Jesus
himself. What has happened to all your joy? I can testify that,
if you could have done so, you would have torn out your eyes
and given them to me. Have I now become your enemy by tell-
ing you the truth? (Galatians 4:8, 9, 13-16)

After Paul left Galatia to tell people in other parts of the empire about Jesus, the Judaizers slipped into town and began poisoning the minds and hearts of the people. They were probably subtle at first, but soon, they openly challenged Paul's authority and message. To win personal power and prestige, the religious elite wanted to destroy the people's experience of grace and replace it with a set of laws to follow. Paul again showed the motives of the Judaizers and pleaded with the people:

Those people are zealous to win you over, but for no good. What they want is to alienate you from us, so that you may have zeal for them. It is fine to be zealous, provided the purpose is good, and to be so always, not just when I am with you. My dear children, for whom I am again in the pains of childbirth until Christ is formed in you, how I wish I could be with you now and change my tone, because I am perplexed about you! (Galatians 4:17-20)

I can almost hear Paul asking them, "How in the world could this happen? You loved me so much you would have pulled out your eyes to give to me, and I love you so much I was willing to be stoned and left for dead to bring Jesus to you! Somehow, these Judaizers came in and turned you against me, but it's not too late—it's never too late to turn back to Jesus. I'm not your enemy. I'm your best friend, and in fact, I'm your spiritual father."

> I can almost hear Paul asking them, "How in the world could this happen?

Maybe the Galatians took Paul's love for granted. Maybe he had taught them so well about grace and he had demonstrated the love of God so well that they assumed he'd just "let it go." This happens in families, and sometimes in churches. Rigid rules and anger aren't fertile soil for relationships. When parents, bosses, or others in authority want power at all cost, they leave the wreckage of collateral damage in their wake. Selfish motives were the first question Paul addressed, but the issue of motivation is woven throughout his letter. Power and control are demonically attractive, but they ruin everyone involved. Paul wasn't willing to let their slide continue. He shined a big light of truth on the Judaizers' motives and message, and he called the Galatians to think long and hard about the direction of their lives. Most of all, he reminded them that his harsh words of correction came from a heart full of love for them. They'd seen it before, so they had every reason to believe it now.

ADMITTING FAILURE

Paul's letter confronts the readers about their failure to stay strong in God's grace; sometimes, we need to hear and speak the truth about our personal flaws. I asked some friends to tell me the most difficult truths they've ever had to tell anyone. They said:

- "Mom and Dad, I'm going to have an 'F' on my report card."
- "Our whole family has asked you to come to tell you that you have a problem you haven't been willing to admit. You're an alcoholic, and it's time for you to get treatment."
- "Mom, I'm pregnant."
- "I'm addicted to prescription pain pills, and I can't stop taking them."
- "You're not doing your share of the work around here. We're going to have to make a change."
- "I don't want to go out with you anymore."
- "There's not enough money to pay the bills. In fact, we

haven't had enough for a long time. We're buried in debt, and I don't know what to do."

- "Dad, I got a speeding ticket. It's going to cost $185."
- "I can't be your friend. You're doing things I don't want to do."
- "I've been watching you, and it seems you're going backwards. I'm very concerned about your spiritual condition."

Speaking the truth—about others or about ourselves—requires a large dose of courage. When we've spoken up in the past, it may not have gone very well. We got clobbered! It cost a friendship, a job, or even the love of people in our family. We were trying to do the right thing, but it was a disaster. We even prayed about it, but God didn't seem to be listening. Now, even thinking of having another conversation like this makes our palms sweat and our mouths dry. We're afraid of what we might lose.

> Speaking the truth—about others or about ourselves—requires a large dose of courage.

LISTEN TO TRUTH-TELLERS, BE A TRUTH-TELLER

Paul told the Ephesians that God wants us to "speak the truth in love" (Ephesians 4:15) to one another. Quite often, the truth is wonderfully affirming. We speak words of love and encouragement. Paul's letters are full of truth about the nature of grace and our new position as loved, adopted, forgiven children of God. But from time to time, the truth hurts. Paul's letter to the Galatians is a prime example of this type of honest communication. The goal isn't to crush or harm in any way, but to correct and build. Three principles help us understand and communicate this kind of truth:

1. Truth divides.

When we speak the truth to someone, we force a decision: Some like it, but some don't. Some people are glad to obey, but others resist and run away. When I teach that every soul matters to God, some people bow their backs and ask defiantly, "Yeah, but what about . . . ?" They fill in the blanks with people they don't respect. When we have preferences and prejudices, we aren't like our Lord who welcomed everyone who was willing to come to Him. God has called us to be like the Good Samaritan and care for people who are hurt and broken, people of all ages, classes, races, religions, and backgrounds. When we represent "the big tent" of the gospel of inclusion, some self-righteous people can't stand it. This truth divides us.

When I've taught that every person is valuable to God, some people have gotten so upset they've left our church. They look for another church where everyone looks just like them. Their attitude is selfish: "I'm not going to worship with *those people!* I'm going to find people who make me feel more comfortable." But their ignorance and hard hearts don't change God's truth that all people are welcome in the kingdom of God if they trust in Jesus.

When we unapologetically say that Jesus is the only way to God, others reject us as being too narrow and judgmental. That's okay. We're in good company. Jesus clearly claimed to be the "I Am," the Jehovah God of the Old Testament, and look where it got Him—they killed Him for it.

A person may solemnly assert, "I don't believe in gravity," but he can't avoid living as if it's true.

Another may claim, "God doesn't really love me," but that heartfelt perception doesn't alter the reality that God demonstrated His love in a bold and dramatic way when Jesus paid the ultimate price to rescue us.

And today, in our postmodern world, many people proclaim, "I think there are many ways to God. All religions are basically the same, and everyone ends up in the same place." That's a very interesting philosophy because none of those religions agree with this statement. Being so open-minded is really being empty-headed. It doesn't change the truths about God, the promised Messiah, and the cross of Christ—which clearly say He is the only way to God. Over and over again, Jesus made categorical claims to be God in the flesh. He didn't leave the door open for any other interpretation. That's why they arrested and executed Him. In His day, the cross of Jesus divided people between believers and unbelievers. It still divides us today.

2. If you tell the truth, you'll have enemies.

I've known some people who have delighted in blasting people with truth, and they felt powerful when they destroyed people with their arguments. That's not love. It's manipulative, dominating, cruel power. But even when we speak the truth with care, love, and patience, some will despise us for intruding into their world. Right motives and wise words don't guarantee a repentant response. We speak as clearly and lovingly as we can, and we leave the results to God.

If we genuinely love people, we'll be bold to tell them what they need to hear even if they don't want to hear it. I'm not a very popular counselor because I refuse to tell people what they want to hear. If they come to hear the truth, they'll get it. But if they come to be affirmed in their sins or foolishness, they'll be deeply disappointed. Out of sincere love for people, I've said, "What you're doing is sin. If you continue on this path, it'll cause more heartache for you, you'll be a poor example for those around you, and God can't bless you if you're turning away from Him and His will. Please choose Him. He'll forgive you, restore you, and put you on a path of wholeness and purpose." Sometimes, people's hearts have melted and they repented on the spot. Often, they've gone away to think about it a while, and they eventually turned back to God. But too often, they've rejected me, my message, and my God—and in their anger, I've become their enemy. It's deeply troubling to plead with people to turn to God from their sin, but instead, they see us as their enemies because we've told them the truth.

> If we genuinely love people, we'll be bold to tell them what they need to hear even if they don't want to hear it.

The question each of us needs to ask is this: Is it worth diluting or avoiding the truth to remain a friend? A second question provides the answer: Am I really a person's friend if I avoid speaking the truth even if it hurts? If we truly love people, we'll tell them the truth. If we avoid the truth, we become enablers. This term is most often associated with the family members of addicts.

A spouse, parent, or child refuses to confront the addict's behavior and rationalizes: "He won't do it again," "She can't help it," or "Who would care for him if I don't?" But enabling someone is lying—to ourselves and to that person. An enabler is unwilling to take the risk to speak the truth, the risk of being ridiculed or abandoned by the person whose life is out of control. And an enabler believes she is helping the addict by avoiding the painful truth—so this avoidance seems like the epitome of love for the addict. Actually, enablers take sides with the addict against anyone else who tries to speak the truth.

Of course, this principle applies far more broadly than alcoholism and drug addiction. We may avoid the hard truth about people of any age who are acting in self-destructive, irresponsible ways, but our enabling reinforces their behavior, prolonging and deepening the problem.

3. If you make truth-tellers your enemy, you'll be blinded to the truth.

Not only do we need to *be* truth-tellers, we also need to *listen to* people who tell us the truth. Sooner or later, if we resist and avoid truth, people will stop being honest with us. At that point, we live in a self-constructed fantasy world of liars, deceivers, and enablers, and we hear only what we want to hear. This is a common phenomenon in the families of addicts. They've lived with the lie so long they don't even know what's true any more.

Several years ago, I wore a new tie on a Sunday morning. I picked it out because I thought it was strikingly handsome. When I came off the stage after the first service, our media director,

Chris Lesher, met me at the door. He asked, "Pastor Rod, is that a new tie?"

I was thrilled that he'd noticed. I smiled proudly, "Yes. Yes, it is."

Chris reached out his hand and said, "Pastor, please give it to me." As I took it off and gave it to him, he said, "Pastor, never wear that tie again. It showed up like a test pattern on the screen." And he walked back to his booth.

Was I angry with Chris? Not at all. I'd much rather have him tell me my tie distracted the people in the audience than to cling to my beloved piece of cloth. I *needed* to know the truth, and I *wanted* to know the truth.

One Sunday night, we had a wonderful service, but it went a bit long because so many people came to the altar to do business with God. As I walked out of the building with my son, Tyler, I couldn't contain my enthusiasm. I told him, "Wasn't that a great service, son?"

He gave me that knowing smile kids give their parents and said, "Yeah, Dad, it was a good service, but it was too long."

I reacted a bit defensively, "But it was because so many people came forward for prayer."

He answered, "No, it was long because you wasted too much time earlier in the service. Dad, please don't do that again."

I was stung, but I immediately knew Tyler was right. I didn't like hearing the truth that night, but I needed to hear every word.

When we make truth-tellers into enemies, we eliminate our best source of honest feedback, and we short circuit a primary path of repentance. The truth may hurt, but not knowing the truth hurts much, much more.

Invite truth-tellers into your life, and value them like gold! Sometimes, we block the people God has put in our lives, and everyone suffers. Our spouse, children (especially grown children, but even kids can speak truth to us), good friends, and spiritual leaders are watching us and have access to our lives. If we let them, they can give us countless midcourse corrections before we drift too far off God's path. When they tell us things we don't want to hear, we need to avoid reacting defensively. They aren't our enemies! They're speaking the truth in love to build us up, not to destroy us. If we get angry, we need to apologize. We might say, "What you said hurt my feelings, but I really needed to hear it. I'm sorry for reacting to you so negatively. Please, forgive me. Keep telling me the truth. I need to keep growing, and I can't grow without your love, support, and honesty."

> When we make truth-tellers into enemies, we eliminate our best source of honest feedback, and we short circuit a primary path of repentance.

TEST THE CRITICS

It may be difficult to hear the truth from someone who genuinely has our best interests in mind, but it's very hard to respond with an open heart when we believe someone is trying to control and dominate us. How can we tell the difference between loving truth-tellers and those who are manipulative? Ask these questions:

1. Do they love me and have my best interests at heart?
2. Have they proved their love for me over the long haul?
3. Is what they're saying consistent with Scripture? (Scripture is

our objective standard of truth. All perceptions must line up with God's truth.)

4. What's their track record with others? Are they known as truthful, loving, and helpful in other relationships?

5. What's their motive? Is it redemptive or selfishly controlling?

It's helpful to have a quick comparison of the two kinds of critics who confront us—and to evaluate ourselves as we speak truth to the people around us. Generally, we can identify two categories: destructive critics and constructive ones. Let's take a look:

Destructive Critics	Constructive Critics
Talks to others (gossip)	Speaks to the person
Attacks character	Addresses behavior
Is abusive	Is redemptive, helpful, and loving
Becomes increasingly harsh	Becomes increasingly supportive
Changes the attack	Is consistent
Stays at arms-length	Is involved in the process of restoration
Delights in fault-finding	Delights in restoring
Is emotionally charged	Is logical and reasonable
Is vague in accusations	Is specific
Exaggerates for effect	Speaks unvarnished truth
Is a taker	Is a giver

Constructive critics are gifts from God. Their goal is to equip, to strengthen, to redirect us so we follow God's path. When they say hard things, they have a tear in their eyes and love in their hearts. Their love and wisdom win our trust, and we invite them to give us input. When my administrative assistant tells me I've received a call from a destructive critic, I groan and dread picking up the phone. But when I find out a constructive critic has called me, I gladly call that person back.

Paul was a constructive critic—for the Galatians and for us. His motivation wasn't to grind people into the dust, punish them for disagreeing with him, or dominate them with his authority. He pleaded with them to come back to Jesus. When our motives are right, we can say very hard things, but we should say them with a tender heart.

> When our motives are right, we can say very hard things, but we should say them with a tender heart.

People who live by rules are often narrow, angry, destructive critics. They're mad at themselves for failing to live up to the standards, and they're mad at others who fail to live by them—which is everybody. Jesus had plenty of destructive critics. They found fault with Him for virtually everything He said and did. They condemned Him for His kindness to heal people on the Sabbath, and they criticized Him for hanging out with the misfits of His day. They were outraged that He loved Gentiles, women, children, and tax gatherers. And they were furious when He talked about the vast love of God for all people. How mad were they? They conceived a plot to kill Him, and they pulled it off. It's my hunch that many (and probably all) of the people who are destructive critics have a serious grace deficiency. If they would experience the incredible love of Jesus, their view of others would change. They'd begin to love the unlovely, accept the unacceptable, and sparingly and graciously correct those who need to be reminded about God's path for their lives.

We have to be careful to avoid labeling people as "destructive critics" just because we don't like what they say. Labeling is a defense mechanism to avoid painful truth. Be courageous enough to listen without instantly dismissing the person or the message. Quite often, the words of even our harshest critics contain a hint of truth. If we dismiss their whole message, we miss a needed correction that God wanted to use to transform us and redirect us. Recently, a man sent me a letter to tell me, "Pastor, you seem so full of yourself." I didn't like reading that letter. It was mean-spirited and bordered on being genuinely abusive. Still, instead of tossing it aside, I prayed about it. As I prayed, the Lord showed me that He is always in the process of purifying my motives. They won't be completely pure this side of heaven. Every day, I ask God to work deeply in my heart to reveal the desire for man's approval instead of seeking His alone, but I'm a work in progress. When I read the letter, I prayed, "God, help me see if this man is right. Show me anything that is a hidden motive for man's applause." As I prayed, God showed me some self-focused desires I hadn't noticed before. With a fresh sense of God's grace, I could write the man to thank him for his letter. Although he had meant his letter to hurt me, God had used it to shape me a little more.

People in the public eye are easy targets. Not long ago, I felt particularly stung by a woman's criticism. As I thought and prayed about it, I wanted to run away. I thought, *What kind of job can I do that wouldn't incur anyone's negative opinion?* I quickly realized that every role in our culture—from president to parent, jailor to janitor, farmer to framer—takes heat from time to time. It's part of being human.

All of us are susceptible to attacks from destructive critics. In the last few years, I've noticed that many of them use email instead of speaking directly to the person, they attack a person's character instead of assuming the best and pointing out a concern with a behavior, they bring up things that aren't specific, and they seem to spend a great deal of time carefully crafting the meanest thing they can say. They want to hurt, not help. I've received a few of these emails in the middle of the night. For a while, I checked them and responded as soon as they came in. I don't do that any more. I never check emails after I go to bed because that's when the destructive critics howl at the moon—and at me!

In the Christian community, however, very few people are overtly harsh and critical. We've perfected the subtle art of passive-aggressive communication. We can destroy with a smile! As I listen to conversations, I sometimes hear these manipulative statements:

• "Everybody is upset with you."

 Somehow, our anger at someone is more justified if we couch it in groupthink. Instead of owning our own anger, we globalize it far beyond what is reasonable and true. What we really mean is that *I've convinced three friends to join me in my anger.*

- "Everybody is talking about you."

  We've told a couple of people our side of the story and enlisted their support.

- "Nobody likes you."

  I don't like you.

- "Here's a prayer request about Jim."

  I want to gossip about him, but I don't want to look too obvious.

- "Bless her heart."

  She's an idiot.

- "Do you have a minute? I want your advice."

  I'm about to ruin the next two hours of your life with boring conversation.

- "I'm not trying to be critical."

  I don't even have to try—it comes naturally.

Do you see how all these work? They avoid being direct and honest by deflecting, dissembling, and globalizing. They insist "everybody" agrees with the criticism, and they say things they don't mean. Passive-aggressive communication is dishonest. Avoid it. Take the risk of speaking the truth or keep your mouth shut. (Option B is often a good one.)

THE RISK OF BEING HONEST

Not long after I became a pastor, I received a series of phone calls from Michael, a man in our church. It didn't take long to see a pattern: Every call was a complaint about my preaching, the building, a program, or something else. His voice was very pleasant, but the message was unmistakable: Pastor, you need to change.

Soon my reaction was the opposite of Pavlov's dog. Every time I saw his name on my caller ID, I cringed. For weeks, I prayed that God would give me the wisdom and courage to talk to Michael about his attitude. I felt God wanted me to talk to him for his sake, and I wanted love to show through in the conversation. Finally, on a Saturday morning, I worked up the courage to call him. I was nervous and afraid. I didn't know how he would respond. Would he and his family leave the church? Would he blow up at me? I had no idea.

When the conversation started, my voice was trembling. I began, "Michael, I love you, but I want you to know that when I see your name on my caller ID, I groan. Do you know why?" He was silent. "Because I know you're going to complain about something and correct me. I want you to know that your negative attitude isn't a blessing to me."

He was very quiet. I took a deep breath, and I continued, "I have a suspicion that if you ask your wife, and maybe some others, they'll tell you the same thing."

Our conversation didn't last long. I said what I wanted to say the way I thought God wanted me to say it, and we parted amiably. Michael told his wife what I'd said, and she said, "Pastor Rod is right. You treat me the same way." She told him that she and their two children were tired of being corrected all the time.

To his immense credit, Michael changed. He asked God to transform his heart and his words, and God answered his prayers. He had been a harsh and frustrating critic, but he has become one of my most valued friends, supporters, and board members.

Today, when I see Michael's name and number on my caller ID, I can't wait to answer it. I know I'm going to talk to a man who loves God, loves his family, loves me, and loves the mission God has given him.*

It doesn't always turn out this well, but when it does, it's marvelous to see.

CONSIDER THIS . . .

1. When was the last time someone spoke hard truth to you? How did you respond?

---

*When I sent this part of the chapter to Michael to get his feedback and permission to use it, he sent a reply that speaks volumes about the transforming power of honesty. He wrote, "Rod, I wish I could talk personally to every person reading your book—every pastor and every parishioner. For me the story is so much bigger than any reader could understand. Without that Saturday morning call, I very well could have lost everything that really matters in life. Five years later, God used you to lead me through the most frightening crisis of my life to freedom that I didn't really believe was possible. Without the mutual respect that comes from honesty and openness, relationships don't work. I don't think that a pastor can minister healing in a time of crisis, especially when people need to hear the tough words of Scripture in the face of the sin that entangles them. It's hard enough to hear those words, but we can listen and respond if we know that we have a relationship built on love and respect. Walking through confrontation, repentance, forgiveness and restoration with you in 2003 made the journey in 2008 possible. Thanks for being obedient to God's voice and your calling."

2. When was the last time you confronted someone about a bad attitude or misbehavior? How did it go?

3. What was the context of this question in Paul's letter (Galatians 4:8-20)? What were the reminders he included? What was his tone? What exactly is he asking?

4. What are some ways that truth divides?

5. How would you define and describe an enabler? Have you witnessed one in action? What were the results?

6. How does making truth-tellers into enemies cause us to be blinded to the truth?

7. Look at the contrast between destructive and constructive critics? Which one best characterizes your input into others' lives? Which category would your spouse, kids, and best friends put you in?

8. What are some reasons being passive-aggressive is more attractive than being honest? How does this kind of communication affect relationships?

9. Do you welcome truth-tellers or avoid them? Explain your answer. Take some time to pray about your response to those who tell you the truth and listen to the Spirit to see if He wants you to speak truth to anyone. Be obedient.

7

A TRUE FRIEND

Question #3:

Have I now become your enemy by telling you the truth?

Several years ago on a Friday afternoon, I played golf with my friend, Jim Rodgers. It had been a long, hard week, and it was great to relax with him. As I remember the game, I was soundly trouncing him (but his memory may be a little different). As we walked off the eleventh green, my cell phone rang. I didn't get it out of my bag in time to answer it, so I listened to the message. It was a man who had left our church a few months before. I considered him to be a troublemaker. Jim and I both heard the message: "Pastor Rod, I need to talk to you today. God has been dealing with me. Please call me."

I put the phone back in my bag, grabbed my driver for the twelfth hole, and began taking some practice swings. I noticed Jim looking at me, so I asked, "Yeah, what?"

Jim said simply, "What's wrong, Rod?"

I shrugged, "The call was from a guy who has been a big hassle to me. He and his family left the church. He wants me to call him back." I paused for a second, and then I announced, "You know, we're a lot better off with him gone. I don't even want to return his call."

I could sense the tension building in the quiet of the golf course. Finally, Jim stood next to me and said with more than a tinge of sarcasm, "Rod, that's a great attitude for a pastor. I thought you taught about God's love and forgiveness. Maybe instead of thinking about this hole, you should ask God to fix your attitude."

Instantly, I knew Jim was right. I called the man back and made an appointment to meet at my office as soon as both of us could get there. To my surprise, the meeting I didn't want to have turned out to be a celebration of God's grace and restoration. He had called to apologize for his attitude about me. The ex-troublemaker came back to the church and became an enthusiastic supporter. I'm very grateful for Jim's courageous honesty and his role in my attitude correction. I almost missed a great blessing.

I'm ashamed to tell this story, but it's instructive. I needed someone who loved me enough to gently—or maybe not so gently—challenge my attitude. I've never forgotten the lesson I learned on the twelfth tee that afternoon: It doesn't matter what anyone has said or done to me—I get to choose my attitude.

THE RISK

Jim took a risk to confront me that afternoon. It's always a risk to tell people the hard truth about their attitude or behavior.

When Paul wrote the Galatians, he put it all on the line. He became vulnerable, pleading with them to respond to his love. If he'd been more guarded, he could have just written them off and avoided any relationship with them, or if he had wanted, he could have remained superficial.

When Paul wrote the Galatians, he put it all on the line. He became vulnerable, pleading with them to respond to his love.

He didn't. He begged and pleaded. He pushed and pulled. His language was both fierce and tender. What was the risk? How do teenagers respond when a person is too vulnerable? They make fun of him. The Galatians could easily have done that with Paul. I can almost hear them say, "Look at Paul's letter. What a wimp! He's so angry, but then he's so lame. He thinks he has the ability to make us respond the way he wants, but not any longer. We're done with him!"

A fascinating book is called *The Wisdom of Crowds*. The author, James Surowiecki, explains how the best leaders welcome dissenting opinions and disagreements so the group can hammer out the best option. Instead, many groups—in business, government, churches, and families— practice "the foolishness of crowds" by telling people only what they want to hear. Jesus exposed Himself to the critics in His world, and they took full advantage of it. They made fun of Him, ridiculed Him, and finally crushed Him into the dust. He was willing to be completely vulnerable—physically, emotionally, spiritually, and relationally—at the cross. Why? So he could convince us of His immense love for us.

We use the full range of different forms of rationalization to keep from being vulnerable. Here are a few:

"He won't listen to me."

We've tried to talk to our spouse, kids, parents, co-workers, bosses, or friends before, and they blew us off. Once should be good enough!

"Surely, somebody else would do a better job. In fact, I'm sure someone is already thinking about it."

We excuse ourselves from responsibility by pretending another person will step up. They may, but they may not.

"Who am I to confront anybody? I'm certainly not perfect! It's not my place."

All of the directives to "speak the truth in love" are for flawed people like you and me. No one is exempt.

"I'm not willing to lose the relationship."

Is this the real risk? Not usually. We make grand statements like this to make it seem like the world will come to an end if we speak up. Actually, the world has a better chance of coming to an end if we don't. Many people would rather let a person destroy his life than take a risk of momentary conflict or ridicule.

"I could be wrong."

Yes, it's true. We shouldn't confront people at the drop of a hat, but if we have seen a clear pattern and can point out dates and events of wrongdoing, we can be confident we're on the right track.

NATHAN'S COURAGEOUS LOVE

One of the best examples of truth-tellers is Nathan, a prophet who lived at the time King David ruled Israel. When David was a boy, he had been a forgotten, ridiculed son in his family, but God had other plans. He sent Samuel to anoint the strong, bright young shepherd to take over the kingdom from the first king, Saul, who had proven he wasn't up to the challenge. David's military strength and political savvy were rivaled only by his deep love for God. Everything he touched turned to gold . . . until one day, he touched someone else's wife. In the season when kings went out to war, David stayed home. One evening, he was looking over the parapet of his roof, and he saw a beautiful woman bathing on the rooftop next door. He should have had his mind on his business, but instead, he sent for Bathsheba and committed adultery. And she got pregnant.

> It's human nature to keep sin a secret—or at least to try to keep it hidden. But keeping secrets is deadly.

It's human nature to keep sin a secret—or at least to try to keep it hidden. But keeping secrets is deadly. Our friends in the recovery movement often say, "We're only as sick as our secrets." Most people go to great lengths to hide some sin or flaw behind a mask of smiles, a façade of success, or a brick wall of denial. Some people do almost anything to maintain the cover up. To hide his sin, David tried to get Bathsheba's husband, Uriah, to come in from the war to have sex with her, but he was too noble to enjoy his wife while his comrades were in danger. Plan A failed, so

David moved to Plan B. He asked Uriah to stay one more night. David gave him enough alcohol to get him drunk, hoping he'd give in and have sex with his wife. The next morning, David saw him sleeping at his front door. Even drunk, Uriah wouldn't go in to be with his wife. Now, David concocted Plan C. He wrote a battle plan for his commander and sent it with Uriah back to the battle lines. The order was to send Uriah's regiment forward where they would be under heavy fire and then pull back, leaving him exposed to enemy fire. It worked, but there was collateral damage. Uriah was killed along with many other brave men beside him.

Finally, David was free to marry Bathsheba. He thought his sin was now a complete secret. But God knew. God doesn't wink and nod when we choose to walk away from Him. He graciously puts up barriers and reminders for us to come back to Him. Quite often, the biggest and brightest red flags of warning are natural consequences. David's sinful behavior initiated a cascade of tragedies in his family: the loss of two sons, the rebellion of another, the ridicule of the people, and intense guilt and shame.

All around us, we clearly see the consequences of personal sin. Why are we so slow to be honest about our faults and flaws? There may be a hundred reasons, but these three are the most common:

Fear

We imagine saying to a friend or family member, *If you knew what I'm really like, you wouldn't like me anymore. If you knew what I've done, there's no way you would want to be around me. If you knew the truth about me, our relationship would be over. I'm afraid of the consequences if you find out.*

Insecurity

Our secret, private conversation goes like this: *If you knew what I have done, you'd reject me. You wouldn't want me as a friend, a husband, or a church member. You'd kick me to the curb.*

Pride

Our mental gymnastics are: *If you knew the truth, you would lose respect for me. You'd never see me the same way again.* Our pride produces a false sense of identity and security. The thought of someone losing respect for us is enough to make us believe it's worth it to cover up anything that causes us to lose face.

About a year after Uriah was killed and David married Bathsheba, God sent Nathan on a dangerous mission: to confront the king about his sin. Why did God have to send the prophet? Because David had stopped listening to God and obeying Him. One of the consequences of his sin was that he had forfeited his intimate relationship with God. Nathan had a tough assignment, but he was very shrewd in how he communicated with David. He told him a story about two men. A rich man had lots of sheep and cattle, but a poor man had only one little ewe lamb, and he loved the lamb with all his heart. When the rich man wanted to prepare a feast for a friend, he didn't want to kill and cook one of his hundreds of lambs, so he took the poor man's lamb from him.

David got the point of the story. His anger burned at the rich man. He growled at Nathan, "As surely as the LORD lives, the man who did this deserves to die! He must pay for that lamb four times over, because he did such a thing and had no pity" (2 Samuel 12:5-6).

Nathan's trap was set. He looked straight at David and replied, "You are the man!"

Can you imagine how vulnerable, exposed, and ashamed David felt at that moment? He could have grabbed a spear and run Nathan through, but he didn't. He stood there and took his medicine. Nathan then delivered God's message:

> This is what the LORD, the God of Israel, says: "I anointed you king over Israel, and I delivered you from the hand of Saul. I gave your master's house to you, and your master's wives into your arms. I gave you the house of Israel and Judah. And if all this had been too little, I would have given you even more. Why did you despise the word of the LORD by doing what is evil in his eyes? You struck down Uriah the Hittite with the sword and took his wife to be your own. You killed him with the sword of the Ammonites" (2 Samuel 12:7-9).

What was God saying to David? He was reasserting His authority over his life and reminding the king of his background. Nathan then told David about the severe consequences of his sin. He described in detail the pain he would suffer, but again, David didn't come unglued and try to harm the prophet for delivering God's message. David's cover up was blown. He told Nathan, "I have sinned against the LORD." He didn't blame Bathsheba for taking a bath on the roof of her house, and he didn't accuse Uriah of treachery for not having sex with his wife. He didn't pass the buck to God and blame him for failing to control his sexual appetite or murderous urges. He simply confessed his sin, and God graciously forgave him. Don't misunderstand: David still experienced the consequences of his sin, but God forgave him. Both can be—and often are—true for us, too.

Paul would have looked at this history lesson as a perfect example of what it means to be a true friend—loving people enough to tell them the truth. That's what he did for the Galatians, and that's what God wants us to do with the people in our lives. Later in this letter, Paul gives a very practical application. He wrote, "Brothers and sisters, if someone is caught in a sin, you who live by the Spirit should restore that person gently. But watch yourselves, or you also may be tempted" (Galatians 6:1). When we see people drifting (or sprinting) away from God's design for their lives, it's a call to step in and restore them to God's path. We don't jump to confront every time we see someone slip. We look for patterns of established behavior. Our goal isn't to expose and condemn the person, but to restore. It's not to punish, but to build. Our motive isn't revenge, but love. If we enjoy correcting people, there's something very wrong with our own hearts! Instead, we go with compassion, clearly and boldly pointing out the pattern we see and inviting the person to come back to the Lord.

> Our goal isn't to expose and condemn the person, but to restore. It's not to punish, but to build. Our motive isn't revenge, but love.

CHARACTERISTICS OF TRUTH-TELLERS

We may not have "prophet" written on our business cards, but God wants all of us to follow Nathan's example to gently and boldly correct people who have wandered off base. Let's see how we can be more like Nathan:

1. Truth should be told in person, face-to-face.

I love email, Facebook, and text messaging, but difficult truths should never be communicated electronically. You can't see the other person's reaction, so you can't adjust your tone or respond to non-verbal communication, like body language and gestures. I've learned—the hard way—that people who try to be truth-tellers in emails usually aren't effective in communicating in a spirit of love. They either vent too harshly or are too timid. Too often, they sit behind their computer late at night and spew their venom.

2. The goal of truth telling is redemptive, not punitive.

A truth-teller genuinely wants the hearer to grow and achieve God's purpose. His aim isn't to produce pain or punish the person in any way.

I get some nasty emails, sometimes filled with vicious words that question my motives, my character, my words, and my actions. They often label me in some derogatory way. That's not a truth-teller; that's an attacker! The goal determines the approach.

3. Love is the motivation behind truth telling.

To be honest, it's a lot easier to avoid telling someone hard truths and opt out of difficult conversations. But love compels us to action, to care enough to sit down, face-to-face and say, "I'm concerned about you. I see something in your life that worries me." Love takes courageous action.

4. Prayer should always precede truth telling.

When I need to have a painful talk with someone, I pray, "God, let my observations and suggestions be received in the right spirit. Let my words be laced with love and compassion. Reveal to me if my motive is wrong in any way. Show me how to communicate Your truth in a way that pleases You."

5. Truth telling happens in the context of trust in relationships.

When people know someone loves them and has their best interest at heart, they're more willing to hear the truth. I've learned that sometimes, I need to wait and prove my love before I can have the difficult conversation.

6. Truth-tellers are good listeners.

Some people are eager to condemn others with their observations of their bad behavior, but it's wise to be a good listener. Too often, I've made assumptions about people based on incomplete information. I've done that with Cindy, my boys, friends, and people in our church. When I walk in with a prophet's pronouncement, it shuts off any dialogue. I'm learning to say, "Here's what I'm noticing about your life. Help me out here. Tell me what's going on."

When I invite people to tell their side of the story, they sometimes admit, "You're right. That's exactly what's going on," but often they say, "Well, you got part of it right, but here's what you don't know." And they explain things that help me understand much better. Active listening involves asking good questions and remaining silent while people answer. It doesn't help if we're plotting our next attack while they're answering! And good listening builds trust, which is essential for the present conversation and for the future of the relationship.

If you wonder if you're a good listener, ask your spouse, your kids, your best friends, and those who work with you. You might be surprised by their answers.

7. Truth telling is a huge risk.

Sometimes, I've experienced pain from speaking truth to people. Difficult conversations don't always go well. We hope people will respond like David, but too often, they react very defensively. I've lost a relationship or two, but not because I didn't care about them. I lost these connections because I cared enough to step in and try to make a difference. I've laid my head on the pillow at night and wept over lost friendships, but I knew the relationship would never be rich and real without honesty. I've talked to people about addictions, affairs, and leadership flaws. Some of these conversations have been brutal, but I've been on both sides. People who love me have told me some difficult truths, too.

8. Truth telling is Biblical.

From Genesis to Revelation, God is the ultimate truth-teller. Jesus is called "the Word" because it's God's nature to reveal Himself and His purpose to us—and often, He corrects our misguided lives. Even a casual reading of the Bible shows that God speaks the truth in love to redirect His wayward people, time after time. As we become a little more like Him, we'll follow in His footsteps with loving honesty in our relationships, too.

9. If you're excited about confronting someone with the truth, you're the wrong person!

I've never met people who are good at confrontation and love it. Instead, they pray and think in advance. They anguish over how they'll say particular words and imagine how the person will respond. Finally, they pour themselves into it with all they have. Most of the time, they dread it, but they're relationally invested enough to follow through. Often, they see God work the miracle of repentance and restoration, but sometimes, they watch as people walk away. There are no guarantees when we trust God to become truth-tellers—but we can be sure that we're doing what God has called us to do.

How do we know if we have the character of a "true friend"? We prove we're trustworthy and loving only when we step into people's lives to tell them the truth. Solomon, one of the wisest men who ever lived, observed, "Wounds from a friend can be trusted, but an enemy multiplies kisses" (Proverbs 27:6). In our relationships with family, friends, co-workers, and neighbors, we can't afford to be cowards and enemies. Too much is at stake in their lives and ours. We must learn to be true and trusted friends.

> In our relationships with family, friends, co-workers, and neighbors, we can't afford to be cowards and enemies. Too much is at stake in their lives and ours.

WHAT ABOUT YOU?

Let's look at these principles from the other side. Have you made someone your enemy because he told you the truth? Have you rejected the message and the messenger because the truth was too difficult to hear?

Spouses, parents, siblings, pastors, friends, neighbors, co-workers, and bosses have lovingly confronted some of us. Their motive and approach may not have been perfect, but they spoke the truth the best they knew how. Even then, we pushed them away because we didn't want to face hard facts. Now, we realize our response was misplaced. How do we fix it? How do we get truth-tellers back in our lives? Let me suggest some clear and powerful steps:

1. Ask God to forgive you.

You can pray, "God, forgive me for foolishly thinking I could change the truth by ignoring it. Forgive me for my stubbornness and pride. Forgive me for making truth-tellers my enemies. Thank You for Your wonderful grace and forgiveness! Help me change, Lord."

2. Ask the truth-tellers to forgive you.

You need these people in your life! They stopped telling you the truth only because you quit listening. You know who they are. Ask for their forgiveness. You can tell them, "I want you to know that you were right. You told me my path would lead to heartache. It did. You told me I couldn't continue in sin and not expect consequences. You were right. Please, forgive me for not listening to you. I need you in my life. Thank you for loving me enough to tell the truth."

Some of us need to make a phone call today to have this conversation. We might be afraid and wonder, *But what if they don't receive it? What if they make fun of me for being so stupid?* In the vast majority of cases, they'll be thrilled we called. In the past, they loved us enough to tell the truth, and now, they'll rejoice in the fact we're finally facing it.

3. Act on the truth.

Remember, truth divides. It forces us to see divergent choices and pick a path. If you're an addict, admit it and start the process toward freedom. If you've engaged in a pattern of ongoing sin, admit it and stop it. Take the first crucial step to respond to the truth: admit it.

4. Recognize that the people who love you the most are those who are willing to tell you the truth.

Don't ever be like the people in Galatia and let the Pauls in your life become your enemy simply because they told you the truth. Value these people. Honor them, thank them, and spend time with them. They may have been corrective in the past, but as you prove you've changed, they'll delight to affirm your new choices and your healthy direction.

Occasionally, I hear people claim: "I don't need any people in my life to tell me what's right and wrong. All I need is Jesus!"

My response is that it depends on what you're talking about. If you're referring to salvation, then yes, it only comes through the sacrificial blood of the Savior. Nothing and no one else can add anything to Jesus' payment for our sins. But if this statement is about how a person grows in grace, overcomes self-deception, and takes steps forward to apply God's truth every day, the answer is a little different. God has given us His word, His Spirit, and His people to encourage and guide us. Solomon wrote about the powerful—and often grating—dynamic of relationships: "As iron sharpens iron, so one person sharpens another" (Proverbs 27:17). In the New Testament, Jesus and the writers offer dozens of instructions about how God wants us to build up other Christians. One set of these passages is known as the "one another" verses. They tell us to love one another, accept one another, forgive one another, rebuke one another, support one another, show patience to one another, and on and on. From my own experience and my observation of other believers, I can confidently say that I haven't seen anyone grow in faith without the powerful blend of these three engines of spiritual vitality: the word, the Spirit, and strong relationships with fellow believers. Actually, when people say, "All I need is Jesus," I suspect their pride and fear cause them to avoid meaningful interaction at all cost. Maybe, they were hurt badly in close relationships in the past, or maybe, they have a lot to hide.

> If we want to know Jesus more intimately, and if we want our lives to really count, we have to be in community with at least a few other Christians who have earned our trust by living in grace and truth.

As long as they keep people away, they'll remain islands of ignorance, and their Christian experience will stay stagnant. If we want to know Jesus more intimately, and if we want our lives to really count, we have to be in community with at least a few other Christians who have earned our trust by living in grace and truth.

OVERCOMING FEAR

A lady in our church came to me for some pastoral counseling. When she sat down in my office, she began telling me about her husband's problems. Her goal was to fix him. I make it a policy not to talk about people who aren't in the room, so I asked her to change the topic to her own hurts and desires. She seemed uncomfortable talking about herself. She talked guardedly about some hurts and fears, but I could tell she didn't want to share her deepest secrets with me. That night, however, she decided to write me a letter, telling me about the most painful, shame-filled event in her life. She was terrified that I'd reject her after I read it, but she sent it anyway.

Two days later, her letter arrived at my office. She explained that she felt ashamed and insecure because she'd had an abortion when she was a teenager. I immediately called her and asked to see her. I wanted her to know that I was amazed at her courage and honesty. She was very relieved to hear my response!

As she grew and healed, she became more open about her pain and her experience of God's restoring grace. I asked her if she'd be willing to tell her story in a message, and she agreed. Before the Sunday she was scheduled to share her story, she went to her family to tell them about the abortion. She had kept it a secret for many years, but now, it was time to tell them the truth. She was amazed at their warm and loving response. When she spoke at our church the next week, they were all there to support her. Here's the story in her own words:

> *I was raised in a broken home. My parents divorced when I was 12. With a joint custody arrangement, my sister and I packed our suitcases every Saturday and went to the other parent's home. As my life was shifted back and forth, my spiritual life began to shift, too. As a teenager, I began to rebel. My dad and I weren't close—probably because we are both strong willed individuals, and we didn't have great communication skills. My mom remarried and found herself in an abusive relationship, which affected my sister and me as well.*

> *Insecurity was my constant companion. In high school I was active in basketball, winning "all conference" awards. I actually won my high school beauty pageant, but in my heart I still felt I was a failure.*

> *At 18 years old, I found myself in an abusive relationship. My parents voiced their concerns, but at this point, I couldn't see any way out. Just when I thought things couldn't get worse, they did. I became pregnant. Feeling I could no longer bear the abuse or my child being abused, I made the choice that would change my life forever. Telling no one, I went alone and aborted my baby. Even a year later, I still felt like God totally abandoned me. I felt so alone.*

> *In February of 1990, a young man I had known for eight years came into my life, and ten months later we were married. After a few years, I told Mark about the abortion. We*

wept together. Just as I had done before, we tried to forget it and move on. I knew God had forgiven me, but I didn't realize I needed emotional healing.

For fifteen years, I have had feelings of self-hate, anger, unforgiveness, depression, insecurity, and shame all bottled inside of me. My healing finally began one afternoon after sharing with Pastor Rod. Since then, I have been able to tell my family, and their love has been unreal. I believe we're closer now than ever before.

Looking back over the last year, I can see each step that God has taken me in my healing process. I was a child of God, filled with the Spirit, even working in ministry, but for fifteen years I'd been crippled by my past. Thank God I am finally healed and walking in God's strength!

I now have a passion to see women who need healing and restoration. As God began showing me my assignment, He reminded me of the scripture that He had given me through two ministers on separate occasions. Jesus told Peter, "Satan had desired to sift you as wheat, but I am praying for you, that your faith would not fail, and when you are converted, strengthen the brethren" (Luke 22:31). My heart's desire is to continue to become stronger in Christ and see others healed and restored.

Today, I'm a minister's wife with two beautiful children, and I'm emotionally healed. I know that there are many others who desperately need healing from their past, too. God desires to heal and restore each of us. I am a testimony of God's grace,

healing and restoration, and He desires to do the same for all
of us who are hurting.

Truth telling begets truth telling. As she talked to the people at our church, God opened a floodgate of women who finally found the courage to talk about deep wounds from their past. Some had endured abortions, some had been addicts, and some had emotionally abandoned their children. But the impact wasn't only on women. Men were deeply affected by her forthright honesty, as well. They told about fears and hurts they'd buried long ago, but they realized these problems had affected every relationship and every decision since the day the events took place.

> No one is beyond the forgiving, restoring grace of God. No matter what we've done or where we've been, God welcomes us back with open arms.

To be honest, I'd only spoken the truth I knew when I talked to her in my office that day— that it's good to talk about our own problems instead of someone else's. But God used that conversation to open the door to a much larger truth in her life. Today, she's serving in a ministry to women who are struggling to overcome the guilt they experience because they've had abortions. God is using her in a powerful way to bring hope to the hopeless.

No one is beyond the forgiving, restoring grace of God. No matter what we've done or where we've been, God welcomes us back with open arms. We may experience the natural consequences of our choices, but we can experience God's love and power more than ever before. Fear and pride block God's restorative work in our lives, but all He needs is a barely opened door of honesty and courage to begin a marvelous work to bring light into the darkest recesses of our hearts. Jesus came, John tells us, "full of grace and truth" (John 1:14), and as God's children, we have the unspeakable honor of representing Him with truth and grace in all our relationships. Will you be a truth-teller? Will you listen to truth-tellers who come to you?

CONSIDER THIS...

1. What were the risks Nathan was taking when he confronted David?

2. What are the risks we face when we speak the truth to people to challenge their attitudes and correct their behavior?

3. What are some ways you've seen people (maybe even yourself) rationalize so they avoid telling people hard truths? What were the results?

4. Which one of the characteristics of truth-tellers seems easy
    for you? Why? Which one is most difficult for you? Explain
    your answer.

5. What about you? When was a time in your life (maybe now)
    that you made a truth-teller your enemy? How should you
    respond? When will you make the call to ask for forgiveness?

6. Why is it crucial to go to people in love when we speak hard
    truths instead of wanting to get revenge because they've hurt
    us? What are some differences between loving them enough
    to confront them and desiring to control their behavior?

6. Do you need to play the role of truth-teller? Write a plan to
    prepare yourself for this conversation and ask God for wisdom
    and strength. Then pray that the person will be open to the
    Lord and to you.

8

WALK WELL

Let us not become weary in doing good, for at the proper time,

we will reap a harvest if we do not give up.

Paul's letter to the Galatians is the most intensely personal letter in the New Testament. His spiritual children were acting up, and he wanted to put them back on the right path. At the end of the letter, I can picture him as a loving but concerned dad sending a wayward teenager off to camp for a couple of weeks in the summer. The dad would hold his son by the shoulders, look into his eyes, and with a tone that blends pleading and warning, say, "Son, I hope you have a wonderful time, but don't do anything stupid. Be nice to Jim. Don't set the cabin on fire like you did last summer, and son, please, try to listen to your counselor. You can learn a lot if your heart is open. Will you do that for me?"

The last chapter of Paul's letter is a roller coaster of clear instructions and heartfelt hope. His instructions are the culmination of the three questions asked earlier in the letter, and they make specific application of these principles. I've made it a point to ask these questions every day of my life. As I've made this a spiritual practice, God has used them to remind me of His grace, challenge my self-deception and selfish motives, point me to the Spirit's power, and keep me deeply involved in the lives of people I love. But there's another benefit I've experience: I have more peace and joy than ever before. Earlier in my life, I'd been striving to please people and impress people. I had to win at everything I did, and I desperately wanted the applause of the people around me. The message of Galatians is clear: When these things take center stage in my life, the love and power of God are cut short. As the three questions repeatedly point me back to the vast and deep grace of God, I'm not pushing and striving for personal gain nearly as much. Oh sure, there are still times when the Spirit shows me another dark crevice in my heart that needs the light of God, but I'm so grateful for the freedom and fulfillment I've found in resting in God's magnificent love.

> The three questions also help me redefine success.

The three questions also help me redefine success. A deeper experience of God's grace hasn't made my painful past go away. No matter how I slice it, I was a misfit for my entire childhood. But I no longer wear the label of a loser. God's unconditional acceptance of me, with all my flaws and idiosyncrasies, enables me to use the pain for good instead of letting it haunt me for the rest of my life. In my insecurity, I'd been a compulsive people-pleaser, but increasingly knowing the love of Christ has taken away the fear and replaced it with gratitude and peace. Today, I'm not as defensive or driven, so I'm a better husband, a better parent, a better friend, and a better pastor. I can honestly say that I'm far less concerned about impressing people with my success or my parenting skills—because I'm far more concerned with pleasing the One who has proven His love for me.

Two centuries ago, a pastor named Thomas Chalmers preached a sermon called "The Expulsive Power of a New Affection."[1] This title wouldn't look good on a church marquee today, but it's a great message. He said that real change doesn't come from just trying to get rid of the bad things in our lives. They are only expelled when something greater, more wonderful, more glorious captures our hearts and crowds them out. That's exactly what's happened to me! No matter how much I tried to stop being self-condemning and self-promoting (which strangely happens at the same time in the human heart), my efforts failed. But as the magnificence of the grace of God has increasingly filled my heart, self-hatred and the thirst for people's approval has become less attractive to me. It's a miracle of grace—and it's exactly the reason Paul wrote his letter to the Galatians.

Don't get me wrong. I still have a long way to go, but I'm convinced Jesus is thrilled when I respond to His prompting with a humble, repentant heart. Not long ago, I was invited to speak at a major conference for pastors. As I sat in the audience waiting to be called to the podium, I thought, *If I do well here, there's no telling how far I can go! I'll get invitations to speak all over the country at the biggest churches.* I began imagining the acclaim I'd receive from being such a popular speaker. Thank God, it took a while for them to call my name. During that time, the Holy Spirit began to work on me. The Spirit whispered, "So that's it? This is the reason you serve me—for personal power and acclaim?"

I bowed my head and prayed, "God, forgive me. I want to be completely faithful to my assignment today to preach about Your grace and bring honor only to You. To You, Lord . . . I want all the glory to go to You."

Soon they called me to speak. After I finished, I did something I'd never done before. Usually, the speaker stands around after the message to receive the compliments of the people who come up to talk to him, but during the prayer after my talk, I left the building, walked to my car, and left the city. I'd already given myself all the praise I deserved for one night, and I wanted to be sure I didn't take any more. It's very tempting to program our way to success. Instead, God wants us to have a childlike faith and a childlike delight in honoring our Father who deserves all praise and honor and glory and authority. I'm a sinner and a misfit. The only reason God uses me to change a person's life is the grace of God—which first changes me and then flows through me to touch the hearts of others. Apart from the grace of God and the power of the Spirit, I'm still just that insecure, awkward misfit trying to get some attention.

Being objective about my past and my sinful heart isn't self-flagellation designed to earn God's pity and people's sympathy. It's a constant reminder of where I've come from and how much I depend on God for love, forgiveness, and power every moment of the day. A "broken and contrite heart" delights God, not only on the day we first meet Him, but all day, every day. If I have talents, He gave them to me. If I see Him use me in other people's lives, it's a mark of His incredible grace to use someone like me for His eternal purposes. In a culture that's absorbed with power, riches, and beauty, I have to remember that everything I have, everything I am, and everything I'll ever do is a product of God's amazing grace. I deserve nothing, but I've received incredible riches from the hand of God.

> A "broken and contrite heart" delights God, not only on the day we first meet Him, but all day, every day.

Every day, when I ask myself these three questions, I renew my understanding of grace, I'm reminded that I have to trust in God's power to accomplish His purposes, and I'm committed to truth telling even if it costs me some relationships I value. To keep these commitments and grow deeper in the love of God, I've invited truth-tellers into my life to tell me what I need to hear. These aren't isolated events. I've asked Cindy and the boys to be honest with me, I'm in relationships with some very good friends who are sounding boards for me, and I have a team that gives honest feedback on my messages when I give them transcripts before I speak and then again after, each Sunday. I empower people to speak the truth—the good, the bad, and the ugly—in every area of my life so that gradually, I'm conformed to the image of Jesus.

LAST WORDS

If you'd been sitting in church on the Sunday morning in Galatia in the first century when this letter was read, how would you feel? After all of Paul's stinging rebukes, I'd feel like the scum of the earth. I'd want to crawl away and hide. As a good pastor, Paul understands that his message has been hard to hear, so he begins his closing comments with words of restoration and hope. We already looked at the first verse of Chapter 6 in the last chapter about bringing wayward people back to God. Let's look at it in context:

> *Brothers and sisters, if someone is caught in a sin, you who live by the Spirit should restore that person gently. But watch yourselves, or you also may be tempted. Carry each other's burdens, and in this way you will fulfill the law of Christ (Galatians 6:1-2).*

Had people drifted from grace to follow empty rules? Yes. Had they abandoned Paul and God's love to follow the narrow, legalistic Judaizers? They had. Had a life of laws cause them to feel superior instead of humble? It had. They had really messed up their lives, but Paul didn't throw them away. He invited mature believers to restore anyone who had drifted. He gives two qualifications. First, he tells them to watch their own hearts as they correct others "or you also may be tempted." Tempted to do what? When we step into another person's life to correct him, we're tempted to feel superior. We may not be tempted to sin in the way that person sinned, but the temptation for us is to become like the Pharisees who looked down their noses at anyone who wasn't as righteous as they were. Paul reinforces this principle with the second instruction: to carry each other's burdens. We aren't to stand back and condemn at a distance. If we confront people in love, God wants us to "get under the rock" with them to help them shoulder the burden of change. This means we stay involved, offering encouragement always and advice when it's needed. We provide some resources, but we don't do for others what they need to do for themselves. This can be a tricky balance, but it's one God wants us to find when we step into people's lives. When we are actively, assertively, wisely, and lovingly involved in the process of restoring someone, we're

> This means we stay involved, offering encouragement always and advice when it's needed. We provide some resources, but we don't do for others what they need to do for themselves.

practicing the second great commandment: "Love your neighbor as yourself" (Matthew 22:39). We're doing exactly what Jesus has done for us, and we're following His example.

But like the dad sending his son off to camp, Paul immediately warned the Galatians:

> *If anyone thinks they are something when they are not, they deceive themselves. Each one should test their own actions. Then they can take pride in themselves alone, without comparing themselves to someone else, for each one should carry their own load (Galatians 6:3-6).*

I almost laugh when I read this part of the letter: Encouragement and rebuke. Affirmation and correction. Praise and warning. Isn't this just like a dad? Paul is saying, "When God uses you to change a person's life, remember it's not you—it's God at work. You're still a misfit, but you're God's misfit. And don't look around to see how you stack up against others around you. Look at your own life to see if you're making progress. Be glad if you are. And be sure to take responsibility for your own choices and direction in life."

Paul then connects a lot of the dots he has given them in the letter. Is there a connection between grace and works? You bet, but grace must come first. When our hearts are melted and molded by the love of God, our motivations are increasingly purified and our skills honed. But our freedom in Christ isn't an excuse for laziness. The grace of God drives us and compels us—not for selfish gain, but to please Jesus. Paul explained:

> *Do not be deceived: God cannot be mocked. A man reaps what he sows. Whoever sows to please their flesh, from the flesh will reap destruction; whoever sows to please the Spirit, from the Spirit will reap eternal life. Let us not become weary in doing good, for at the proper time we will reap a harvest if we do not give up. Therefore, as we have opportunity, let us do good to all people, especially to those who belong to the family of believers (Galatians 6:7-10).*

Paul is saying, "I've asked you some important questions. Now, it's time to choose. Don't be stupid. Your choices matter. If you want to please people, follow rules, and dominate people or run from them, your life will be a train wreck. But if you choose God's way—pleasing Him, trusting in the Spirit's power, and engaging in real relationships—the life of the Spirit will overflow from your life. Do you get it?"

But Paul doesn't want to promise more than God intends to deliver. He reminds them that patience is part of the fruit of the

Spirit. Occasionally, we spiritually soar like eagles, but more often, we run the marathon of life, and sometimes, all we can do is take the next step without falling down. Through it all, we trust God to sustain us, equip us, and guide us. One of the marks of true faith, Paul points out, is our love for other Christians—especially those of other races, nationalities, and faith practices. It's easy to affirm those who are just like us, but someday, we'll

> It's easy to affirm those who are just like us, but someday, we'll feast at the banquet of God in His eternal kingdom with people from all generations and all parts of the world. On that day, every shred of prejudice will be washed away.

feast at the banquet of God in His eternal kingdom with people from all generations and all parts of the world. On that day, every shred of prejudice will be washed away. Can we at least have a taste of this unconditional acceptance today? Yes, by loving Christians who are different from us and even disagree with us. Can a Pentecostal really love a Presbyterian? Of course, but only if we want to please God, trust the Spirit's power, and have "iron sharpening iron" relationships.

Paul knew that the people listening to the letter being read to them might have been sitting next to a Judaizer or two. The people faced fierce opposition, so he clarified the choice to show there are two voices calling for their loyalty. He wrote:

> *See what large letters I use as I write to you with my own hand! Those who want to impress people by means of the flesh*

are trying to compel you to be circumcised. The only reason they do this is to avoid being persecuted for the cross of Christ. Not even those who are circumcised keep the law, yet they want you to be circumcised that they may boast about your circumcision in the flesh. May I never boast except in the cross of our Lord Jesus Christ, through which the world has been crucified to me, and I to the world. Neither circumcision nor uncircumcision means anything; what counts is the new creation. Peace and mercy to all who follow this rule—to the Israel of God (Galatians 6:11-16).

Again, Paul shows them the plain facts. "Look around," he's telling them. "You can listen to the people who have led you astray, or you can listen to me. It's your pick. But understand the character of the people who are trying to force you to follow the Old Testament laws. Their motives are power and fear. The most important law they command you to keep, circumcision, is irrelevant. What really matters is a Spirit-changed heart. Grace is the only rule worth following. Rules produce bondage; God's love results in freedom, peace, and mercy. Which do you want?"

Now, near the end of his letter, Paul bares all. When he was with them, he was stoned and left for dead. Surely, he tells them, this counts for something. He wrote, "From now on, let no one cause me trouble, for I bear on my body the marks of Jesus" (Galatians 6:17). Paul had said, "Look around at the Judaizers. Do you want to become like them?" Now he's saying, "Look at me. I've suffered for Jesus and for you. Give me a break! Stop causing me so much trouble!"

Finally, Paul adds the last line. I've received a number of corrective, angry emails and letters, but I've never had one that ended the way Paul signs off in this letter: "The grace of our Lord Jesus Christ be with your spirit, brothers and sisters. Amen" (Galatians 6:18). After all the rebukes and harsh words of correction, Paul asks God's blessing of grace for these people. Even after they had been so disloyal to God and to him, he tenderly calls them "brothers and sisters." He wasn't angry at them, but at their sin. He loved them so much that he poured out his heart to them, and at the close, he wanted to affirm again how much he loved them.

All of God's grace and love and power are available to us, all the time, but some of us just can't see it. A few years ago, I was asked to speak at an event in Colorado. Randy, another pastor at our church, went with me to The Broadmoor, a grand hotel near Colorado Springs. I checked into my room, and then I went to Randy's room to see if he wanted to walk around the beautiful golf course. When he opened his door, I looked inside and said, "My room looks exactly the same, except I don't have a chandelier like this in my room."

Randy offered to switch rooms so I could enjoy the chandelier, but hey, I'm a guy. Chandeliers don't mean that much to me. I shook my head, "Thanks, but I'll stay in my room. No problem."

On the way to the golf course, we stopped by my room for a second. I unlocked the door and we walked in. Both of us stood silently for a few seconds. I could tell Randy was choosing his words very carefully. He said, "Pastor Rod, that's a beautiful chandelier."

It had been there all along, but I hadn't seen it. As we learn to live by these three questions, we look at God and our lives from a different perspective. Clouds of doubt and fear are dissolved in the certainly of God's grace. The mysteries of God aren't as threatening any longer because we're more convinced of His undying love. As our sight clears, we finally perceive things that have been there all along, but we didn't see them—and they're beautiful! We remember affirming words that we couldn't believe when the person said them. We look back and see that God's hand guided us through a difficult and painful time when we felt all alone. We reinterpret failures and realize God taught us valuable lessons through them. We see that we crashed because we were running on empty, but now, things are different as we trust God's Spirit. We are so grateful for people who have loved us enough to tell us the truth even when we didn't want to hear it. Instead of complaining about how rotten things have been, we see the faint trace of God's hand, guiding us even in the darkness. In all of this, we're amazed and thankful.

I DARE YOU

You've read the entire book, and I commend you for your tenacity. We've looked at a lot of principles about God and spiritual life. Thanks for wading through it all. But I'm not quite finished. I want to offer one last challenge: I dare you to apply what you've read. I challenge you to ask yourself these three questions every morning for the next three weeks. Drop out of the daily competition with your peers, and quit living for the applause of those around you. Stop upgrading your possessions to have the biggest, newest, and best stuff on the market. This change can only happen with deep reflection and courageous choices. The handle on change is this set of three simple questions—but they won't be simple to apply. They'll force you to look into the deepest parts of your heart, and they'll enable you to find more grace than you ever dreamed possible.

When I pray these questions, I personalize them:

"God, put a check in my spirit to let me know when I say or do anything designed to give glory to me instead of You. Lord, help me craft my words, my actions, my relationships, and my responses to situations to be pleasing to You. When they don't, let me know it. I want to treat people the way You treat them—with respect, kindness, and honesty."

"God, today, I rely on Your power, not mine. Show me when I'm trusting in my own strength, my ability to manipulate people to do what I want them to do, and my wisdom to figure things out on my own. Apart from You, nothing I do makes any sense or has any value."

"Lord, today, I'm committing myself again to truth—to listen to truth and to speak the truth. Give me so much love for the people around me that I'm eager to notice and affirm the good things in their lives, but also, that I'm willing to say the hard things that need to be said, even at the expense of them walking away from me."

As I pray these questions, I take time to be quiet so I can listen for the Spirit's nudge. Sometimes, He reminds me how He used me the day before, and I'm so grateful. And sometimes, He points out the fact that I face a big challenge during the day. I need to be mindful of these three questions all day so I don't drift away.

If you'll pray these questions and listen to the Spirit, God will turn your life upside down . . . in a good way! You'll experience the love of God more deeply than ever before. You'll see more sin in your life than ever, but you'll be more convinced that you're completely forgiven. God will use you in ways you never dreamed possible, and you'll have richer, deeper, more authentic relationships than ever before in your life. But as you become a committed truth-teller, some people will walk away. It's inevitable. Even if you hone the skills of listening and loving, some people just don't want to be around anyone who is so honest. As you see God work in and through you, you'll have a sense of fulfillment, a soul-deep satisfaction that replaces all the demands and drive that had dominated your life. This isn't arrogance or pride. Humility isn't weakness and self-condemnation. It's a profound sense of peace that you're connected to God's heart and walk in His power and purpose.

> If you'll pray these questions and listen to the Spirit, God will turn your life upside down . . . in a good way!

Finally, you'll have a new benchmark so you can measure life by things that really count. Instead of playing the culture's game of running after more success, pleasure, and approval, you'll live for an audience of One. All you'll care about is pleasing Him so that you hear Him say, "This is my beloved son or daughter in whom I am well pleased," and "Well done, good and faithful servant. Come and share your Master's happiness!"

We usually use the term "drop out" in a negative way, but don't you want to drop out of the rat race of always trying so hard but feeling so empty? Don't you long to drop out of the pressure to be more and do more so you can experience real peace and purpose? Wouldn't it be great to drop out of the guilt and shame of not measuring up, the fear of people finding out you're flawed, and the arrogance of thinking you're better than others when you follow the rules apart from God's grace?

What would your life look like if you lived by God's answers to these three questions? How would it affect your daydreams? How would it make you a better spouse, parent, child, friend, and neighbor?

CONSIDER THIS . . .

1. How might daily reflection on the three questions help us re-define success? How would a redefinition help you?

2. How do these questions inspire both a stronger faith and deeper humility?

3. Read Galatians 6:7-10. How does Paul describe the choice he presents to us? Practically, what does this choice look like in your life today?

4. In verses 11 through 16, Paul again warns the people about the Judaizers. Why do you think they needed to hear it again? What do you imagine might have happened in the church the day this letter was read with the Judaizers sitting in the room?

5. How do you think and feel when you realize God's abundant grace and love have been with you all along even though you may not have realized it and even if you resisted it?

6. What would it look like for you to "drop out" of the culture's values and rat race to have more?

7. Take a minute to paraphrase each of the three questions into your own prayer.

   • Question #1: Pleasing God or pleasing people

   • Question #2: Trusting the Spirit's power or your own efforts

   • Question #3: Making truth-tellers your friend or your enemy

8. Are you committed to respond to my dare and ask yourself these questions for the next three weeks? If you are, what do you expect to happen?

9. How do you think using these questions for the rest of your life will make a significant difference in your relationship with God, your motivation, your family, and the choices you make each day?

10. What is the most important thing you've learned from your study of Paul's questions in his letter to the Galatians?

ENDNOTES

CHAPTER 2

1 "Young people prefer praise to sex, money," Sharon Jayson, *USA Today*, cited on January 10, 2011.

CHAPTER 3

1 Max Lucado, *The Applause of Heaven*, (Word Publishing, 1999), 10-11.

CHAPTER 6

1 Arthur Meier Schlesinger, Jr., Fred L. Israel, *My Fellow Americans: The Inaugural Addresses of the Presidents of the United States*, (Facts on File, 2009), 148.

CHAPTER 8

1 Thomas Chalmers, "The Expulsive Power of a New Affection," cited on www.christianity.com/Christian%20Foundations/The%20 Essentials/11627257/

ABOUT THE AUTHOR

Rod Loy has been in full-time pastoral ministry for twenty-five years. He is currently Senior Pastor at First Assembly of God in North Little Rock, Arkansas, a 99-year-old church. In the last ten years under Rod's leadership, the church has grown to over 3,000 in average weekly attendance on four campuses.

His passion for missions has taken him to forty different countries. First Assembly gives over a million dollars to missions every year and has helped plant more than 1100 churches in sixty-three nations.

Rod's unique approach to leadership has led him to adventures in the "real world," which include working as a volunteer lifeguard at a water park. A former children's pastor, Rod has helped develop the Faith Case curriculum for children and is still actively involved with kids, working as a volunteer teacher's assistant in a low-income, academically-challenged public school.

He and his wife Cindy have been married for twenty-four years and have two boys, Tyler and Parker. The whole family enjoys cheering for the Dallas Mavericks and the Arkansas Razorbacks and going four-wheeling.

The Loys live in North Little Rock, Arkansas.

For more information about First Assembly or ministry resources or to watch services online, go to firstnlr.com.

USING 3 QUESTIONS IN GROUPS AND CLASSES

This book is designed for individual study, small groups, and classes. The best way to absorb and apply these principles is for each person to individually study and answer the questions at the end of each chapter then to discuss them in either a class or a group environment.

Each chapter's questions are designed to promote reflection, application, and discussion. Order enough copies of the book for everyone to have a copy. For couples, encourage both to have their own book so they can record their individual reflections.

A recommended schedule for a small group or class might be:

WEEK 1: Introduce the material. As a group leader, tell your story of finding and fulfilling God's dream, share your hopes for the group, and provide books for each person. Encourage people to read the assigned chapter each week and answer the questions.

WEEKS 2–9: Each week, introduce the topic for the week and share a story of how God has used the principles in your life. In small groups, lead people through a discussion of the questions at the end of the chapter. In classes, teach the principles in each chapter, use personal illustrations, and invite discussion.

PERSONALIZE EACH LESSON

Don't feel pressured to cover every question in your group discussions. Pick out three or four that had the biggest impact on you, and focus on those, or ask people in the group to share their responses to the questions that meant the most to them that week.

Make sure you personalize the principles and applications. At least once in each group meeting, add your own story to illustrate a particular point.

Make the Scriptures come alive. Far too often, we read the Bible like it's a phone book, with little or no emotion. Paint a vivid picture for people. Provide insights about the context of people's encounters with God, and help people in your class or group sense the emotions of specific people in each scene.

FOCUS ON APPLICATION

The questions at the end of each chapter and your encouragement to group members to be authentic will help your group take big steps to apply the principles they're learning. Share how you are applying the principles in particular chapters each week, and encourage them to take steps of growth, too.

THREE TYPES OF QUESTIONS

If you have led groups for a few years, you already understand the importance of using open questions to stimulate discussion. Three types of questions are *limiting, leading,* and *open.* Many of the questions at the end of each day's lesson are open questions.

Limiting questions focus on an obvious answer, such as, "What does Jesus call himself in John 10:11?" These don't stimulate reflection or discussion. If you want to use questions like this, follow them with thought-provoking, open questions.

Leading questions require the listener to guess what the leader has in mind, such as, "Why did Jesus use the metaphor of a shepherd in John 10?" (He was probably alluding to a passage in Ezekiel, but many people don't know that.) The teacher who asks a leading question has a definite answer in mind. Instead of asking this kind of question, you should just teach the point and perhaps ask an open question about the point you have made.

Open questions usually don't have right or wrong answers. They stimulate thinking, and they are far less threatening because the person answering doesn't risk ridicule for being wrong. These questions often begin with "Why do you think . . .?" or "What are some reasons that . . .?" or "How would you have felt in that situation?"

PREPARATION

As you prepare to teach this material in a group or class, consider these steps:

1. Carefully and thoughtfully read the book. Make notes, highlight key sections, quotes, or stories, and complete the reflection section at the end of each day's chapter. This will familiarize you with the entire scope of the content.

2. As you prepare for each week's class or group, read the corresponding chapter again and make additional notes.

3. Tailor the amount of content to the time allotted. You won't have time to cover all the questions, so pick the ones that are most pertinent.

4. Add your own stories to personalize the message and add impact.

5. Before and during your preparation, ask God to give you wisdom, clarity, and power. Trust Him to use your group to change people's lives.

6. Most people will get far more out of the group if they read the chapter and complete the reflection each week. Order books before the group or class begins or after the first week.

TO ORDER MORE COPIES

To order more copies, go to

www.influenceresources.com